C000212248

How to Be a Patriot

Sunder Katwala

How to Be a Patriot

Why love of country can end our very British culture war

Harper
North

HarperNorth
Windmill Green
24 Mount Street
Manchester M2 3NX

A division of
HarperCollins*Publishers*
1 London Bridge Street
London SE1 9GF

www.harpercollins.co.uk

HarperCollins*Publishers*
Macken House, 39/40 Mayor Street Upper
Dublin 1, D01 C9W8, Ireland

First published by HarperNorth in 2023

1 3 5 7 9 10 8 6 4 2

A catalogue record for this book
is available from the British Library

ISBN: 978-0-00-855386-9

Printed and bound in the UK using 100%
renewable electricity at CPI Group (UK) Ltd

This book is produced from independently certified FSC™ paper
to ensure responsible forest management.

For more information visit: www.harpercollins.co.uk/green

For Stacy, Zarina, Jay, Sonny and Indira

Contents

Introduction

My Very British Patriotism

'But where are you *really* from?' Some people find this a clumsy question, if asked in the wrong way, too insistently, or just that little bit too often over the years. Speaking for myself, I have never especially minded being asked it – as long as you could spare the time to listen to a slightly complicated answer.

I was born British. That's the easy bit. An indisputable fact on my birth certificate. Doncaster, Yorkshire, England, Great Britain. My birthright claim to this great country of ours.

My name might make it fairly obvious that I might be a bit Indian too – if not quite obvious enough for those whose playground use of the p-word betrayed a shaky grasp of South Asian geography. Yet I felt at least as Irish as I was Indian, if a little less obviously, since I was brought up as an Irish Catholic, with a mother from County Cork.

I certainly grew up northern, at first. Being born in Doncaster made me eligible to play cricket for Yorkshire under their old county-nativist rules, before they changed them in the 1990s for Sachin Tendulkar and Michael Vaughan. I was never that likely to get the call myself.

Having left Yorkshire at an early age, I identified rather more as Scouse. But was I really a proper Scouser? I had begun a life-long relationship with Everton Football Club by the age of five, but living in Ellesmere Port, Cheshire, on the Wirral, across the other side of the Mersey, I would probably have been called a 'woollyback' in Liverpool proper.

Moving south, with my Scouse accent, to Essex when I was 12 certainly strengthened my sense of identification as a northerner at first, though that changed as my accent softened, as if my voice was gradually drifting southwards over the years.

'Mixed' sounded like a useful label for me. I could happily identify with that. Mixed race, for sure, but hopefully not too mixed up about how to put all of this together. I guess it would be fair to assume that I grew up with some identity issues to work through. National identity seemed naively straightforward at first. I watched the World Cups and the Olympics, supporting my country, without knowing any reason why anybody might ever question why I thought any of that had anything to do with people like me.

My teenage self naturally became more aware that these questions of identity, belonging and race could be pretty fiercely contested. I guess it would have been unlikely, with a back-story like mine, not to develop some kind of interest in history. That looked like it might provide some of the keys for explaining how I came to be me – and it turned out to offer some broader insights into how we, the British today, came to be us too.

Eventually, I came to understand that mine was a very British identity indeed.

After all, my dad may have been born four thousand miles away, in Gujarat in India, not far from the birthplace of Mahatma Gandhi. Yet he had been born a British subject too. He did become a citizen of the new Indian Republic, between his third and fourth birthdays, but he was to become British once again several decades later. As a citizen of the Commonwealth, he could, as a newly qualified doctor, take a plane to Heathrow to look for work in the NHS. It was 1968 – the week after Enoch

Powell made his infamous 'Rivers of Blood' speech asking him not to come, or to go back home if he did. His own father was an ally of Enoch in this respect, offering to support him to set up a medical practice if he came back home, with plans to arrange his marriage too.

But Dad stayed. He had met my mum, who was certainly not born British, in County Cork in the 1940s. Yet, as an Irish citizen, she did not need any passport, permit or visa to take the ferry from Cork to Holyhead, before taking a coach onwards to Portsmouth, to begin her training to be a nurse. 'So, are you coming as an immigrant then?' the ticket inspector asked her, on seeing that she had a one-way ticket. Half a century later, Mum has still never become British. A few years ago she took to flying an Irish tricolour, from a flagpole, in her garden in Essex. That was intended, and apparently received, as a friendly riposte to a neighbour's Cross of St George. Her strong sense of being Irish has not prevented her from voting in every General Election for decades. Ireland may have been independent for a century, but we have never treated it, in law, as just another foreign country.

The more I thought about the whole complex history of India, Ireland and Britain, one simple truth became obvious: I could only really be British. It was not exactly a *coincidence*, the son of an Indian doctor and an Irish nurse, that I was British rather than, say, Belgian or Brazilian. I was hardly going to be anything else.

I was not just the product of that complex British history of Empire, decolonisation and post-war migration, but also a child of the National Health Service, whose seventy-fifth birthday is marked this year, and which had employed many Commonwealth and Irish migrants to Britain as doctors and nurses.

Maybe you couldn't really get much more British than this. That became my way of looking at it anyway, though perhaps not everybody else would agree.

I doubt I would have thought of myself as 'patriotic' as a teenager. But I did definitely feel it get easier to be British. This was partly a generational thing, for those of us who could stake a birthright claim to our British identity. It was not that nobody ever told me to 'go back to where you came from' but I could sarcastically point out that it might be a little bit complicated to work out exactly where you might be sending me. How we thought and talked about what it meant to be British was broadening out across the 1990s. I was very much a Britpop indy kid then (more Pulp than Blur or Oasis in that 90s battle of the bands) and with at least one ear harking back to their 1960s antecedents too. What might have been less anticipated was that English identity was becoming more inclusive too, particularly once football started to change in surprising ways.

Even as a teenager, it had been impossible to miss just how differently the economic and social changes of the 1980s were felt in Merseyside and Essex. The softening of political and social conflict after the departure of Margaret Thatcher, Arthur Scargill and Derek Hatton had begun to generate optimistic talk about a more classless society in the era of John Major and ideas about a stronger sense of community from Tony Blair.

So this whole mixed-race, Indian and Irish, Yorkshire-born, Scouse and Essex version of how to be English and British seemed to me to be increasingly fitting together pretty naturally, from the inside, if this is who you happened to be.

But a funny thing happened after the turn of the century. Britain was not just having one identity crisis but several. Governments were losing public confidence over immigration. The events of 9/11 and 7/7 changed the conversation about integration, and whether multiculturalism was part of the solution of how we live together as a community of communities in a diverse society, or becoming part of the problem too, by paying too little attention to what we all needed to share. Economic divides felt starker once again after a financial crash where the banks were bailed out and the debts borne by those who had done least to cause it. Europe divided us deeply, not just over the choice made in the Brexit referendum but in giving us new 'them' and 'us' labels – 'Remainer' and 'Leaver' – for those misguided idiots on the other side. Identity clashes seemed to be breaking out on every front; culture wars, statues and trans rights – with more new labels. Arguments about political correctness gave way to rows about 'wokeness' offering to link all of these issues up and ask everybody to pick a side.

National identities are supposed to be something that we share. So how much use would it be for me to have gained a secure personal sense of identity if my country started falling apart?

My big question about identity, then, had changed. My foundational question had long ceased to be whether British identity could find a place for people like me. The question of whether ethnic minorities could ever be truly British seemed to have been so decisively answered that I could sometimes find it hard to remember why that had been in doubt. It was certainly clear that not everybody shared my sense of confidence about how far we had come. So the big question for me has become whether or not there is still something that can bind all of us together in this era of the 'culture wars'.

I would not claim to speak for anybody but myself. There may be sixty million different journeys to being British today, including eight million experiences of being an ethnic minority person in this country. Our stories, our perspectives and our views differ – partly because of our different experiences in education and work, or of family, faith or community, or simply the range of different ways we have come to look at the world.

Maybe I had just been dealt a particularly lucky hand. Being mixed race, which had once been talked about in terms of agonising, maybe irresolvable identity dilemmas, had somehow become fashionable – a glimpse of a possible distant future where the sharp edges of ethnic identity somehow blurred.

The luck of the Irish had changed. It was not just that the IRA bombs had finally stopped blowing up pubs following the cease-fire and peace deal in Northern Ireland. The Irish moved from being the butt of the joke to becoming a Celtic Tiger at home and a global brand abroad. Curiously, it now seemed to be much easier to celebrate St Patrick's Day in England with pints of Guinness than to work out if we could extend that to find a way to celebrate St George together too.

The image of India at home and abroad shifted even more dramatically. Instead of it being a notable event if there was an Asian face on the television, *Goodness Gracious Me* began telling the jokes through the other end of the telescope.

But I could also see how the direction of travel seemed to be going in the opposite direction after 9/11 and 7/7 for those who were British Muslim. That social changes often felt slower and less inclusive for many people who were black British. There was also a surly sense of grievance from some – a minority no doubt, and a shrinking one, but a vocal one all the same, especially in the internet era – for whom the very fact of my feeling of identity and status could seem to be the core problem. Did my sense of *possession* of our national identity have to involve the *dispossession* of others? Or could most of us, at least, yet find a way through to something that we do want to share?

If that is the challenge that we face, then I think patriotism could be part of the answer we need. Patriotism can take many forms. It can be angry or hopeful, it can be inclusive or exclusive. It can focus more on the past or the future. I want it to do both, because I feel sure that our Britain is a product of our long history, not some kind of breach and betrayal of it. My own patriotism is not about who shouts about it the loudest or who can wave the biggest flag (though the genius of the design of the Union Flag does make it one of the best in the world). I do put a St George's flag out of the car window every couple of summers, usually more in hope than expectation.

That does not mean that I want to lecture anybody on why they need to feel more patriotic. There is no point in taking part in some kind of performative patriotism if that is not what feels right to you. I do want to set out why an inclusive patriotism can help us to work out what we can share in a society like this. I do want to challenge the idea that we would have a more inclusive society if we just tried to leave patriotism and national identity behind. And I do want to challenge those who need to identify some kind of 'enemy within' to energise their own sense of identity and belonging, whether those targets are one minority group or another, or the young or the old, or simply their political opponents, whether on the left or the right.

The best kind of patriotic spirit can help us to contain, manage and perhaps even transcend some of the social divides and identity clashes that many people fear are making our society feel much more divided than most of us would want.

For all of our current anxieties and divisions, I still feel confident that Britain at heart is a nation more of bridgers and balancers than of culture warriors, even if it does not always feel like that. So we need to put more energy into rediscovering once again a pluralist patriotism – a patriotism of both/and; a patriotism that invites us to get out of our rhetorical trenches and to try to talk it over. Trying to talk it over does not mean, in a democracy, that we will have to find common ground, though sometimes we might find that we can. But it could at least give us more understanding of each other, and perhaps more confidence that we can live together as neighbours with those who don't share our politics, or every aspect of how we look at the world. If that is what most of us want, it can seem harder to work out what we can do to make it happen.

We will see again this year that Britain may well be the most traditional of liberal democracies, certainly when it comes to the ceremonies of our great occasions, such as the funerals and coronations of monarchs. Yet we are also much the most liberal of traditional societies, almost certainly among the most liberal of societies that has ever existed.

That may seem to be a contradiction. But I think it may be the trick of how we make it work and what we have evolved together, better perhaps in practice than in a precisely rational theory. I certainly cannot see the last seven decades as an era of decline or a retreat from past glories. I can enjoy Britain's deep sense of its traditions because I can celebrate how this became a kinder, better society for so many over the late Queen's reign – profoundly so for gay people able to be open about who they loved, or women who sought to pursue a career, or ethnic minority Britons for whom the question changed from who let us in and why, to push back the barriers of discrimination and make opportunities more open than they were.

When we do things together in a society like ours, that will invariably be from choice, rather than conscription. A shared society needs shared rituals, shared moments and shared experiences. Shared moments and shared rituals are powerful precisely because they are voluntary. We should choose to make them matter.

So I would say I am patriotic because I am still an optimist about Britain, not just from instinct, but from my personal experience too. As we embark on a new era, it is up to us all to decide what we want it to mean.

1

Flags: Pride or Prejudice?

Nobody told me – when I was eight – that there was any doubt about whether I could be English or British. The first big national question I was personally aware of was this one: would Kevin Keegan be fit enough to play in the World Cup?

England had qualified for España 82 but their talismanic captain was injured. He was by far the most famous player – the one footballer that every eight-year-old had heard of – and so I was among those anxiously awaiting every medical bulletin.

Maybe I felt English before I felt British, if only by the coincidence of sporting chronology. That first football World Cup I was conscious of came two years before the Los Angeles Olympics of 1984. It was also definitely a big deal in our house that Bucks Fizz won the 1981 Eurovision Song Contest, as the United Kingdom, or 'Royaume-Uni' for those votes cast in French, topped the scoreboard as the jury votes were totted up. My sisters even had copies made of those skirts that could change length mid-song, as my brother and I were pressed into making up a quartet. I remember we watched the Royal Wedding that year too, when I was seven, getting somewhat bored by just how long it went on. I even had a fading Charles and Diana Royal Wedding ceremonial mug several years later.

Like almost everybody else, I certainly had a national identity or two a long time before I ever heard any theories about what patriotism is good or bad for. By the time I was a teenager, I had found out how much it mattered to some people that I should not be considered British. Though, if you were to call me a 'Paki' in the local park or the school playground, you might have got a sarcastic lecture about geography and identity. For some reason, when I was about 13, I thought that 'If my dad's Indian, isn't that like me calling you French, dickhead?' was an absolute zinger of a riposte. I never actually got beaten up, somehow.

Before I found myself thinking through these competing arguments, about what the point or purpose of national identity was, I discovered that I was also living them out in my experiences about whether national identity felt like a source of pride or prejudice, about who was or was not included in it, and on what terms. So I became interested in how and why this sense of belonging was something that it was possible to shift and change.

The case against patriotism – dangerous or meaningless?

The charge sheet against patriotism takes different forms. The primary charge is that it can be dangerous – an atavistic appeal to animal instincts and blind loyalties that will drive war and injustice abroad, and exclusion and xenophobia at home. 'Let's increase our population, expand the size of our territory, build a great empire, raise the national prestige, and bring glory to our flag' is the battle cry of the imperialists of every nation, wrote Kōtoku Shūsui, the early twentieth-century Japanese writer and activist.[1] The world wars of the twentieth century exemplify the dangers of patriotism and nationalism, albeit in slightly different

ways in the shifting debates about their origins and consequences.

Yet these are not the only kind of counter-arguments about
patriotism. Another objection places much less emphasis on the
dangers of patriotism and much more on its irrationality and
meaninglessness. 'How could anybody take pride in a mere accident of birth?' is the central challenge often put.

Another increasingly common critique is that patriotism is too
narrow – a barrier to the internationalism that we should all
want to share. John Lennon's *Imagine* is probably the best-known
public statement in the last century of the argument against
patriotism in favour of a utopian cosmopolitanism. 'Imagine
there's no countries, it isn't hard to do. Nothing to kill or die for,
and no religion too.' That utopian message has appealed to many
people, at least as a song lyric, and a reverie about a perfect world,
or at least a less complicated world. Taken seriously, Lennon's
vision is a rather arid one. Indeed, it is much harder to imagine a
world without countries than the lyric suggests.

The serious arguments against patriotism – that the wrong
kinds of nationalism are toxic and dangerous – must be taken
seriously. They depend on getting the type of patriotism that we
want right. But I am inclined to think that those objections to
patriotism that focus on its meaningless and irrationality merit
less respect. I am struck by how often those who make such arguments, 'a mere accident of birth', regard it as self-evidently a
slam-dunk case that will end the argument. This involves a
remarkable lack of curiosity into why most people everywhere,
in their millions and billions, do not agree.

One of the main flaws of the accident of birth argument is
that it mishears the claim being made about specialness as entail-
ing one about superiority too. We all know that many things can
be special to us without necessarily believing they are superior:
my sense of attachment to my children does not entail believing

that they are superior to those of the neighbours. It is hardly irrational to have a sense of attachment and affection, belonging and pride, in relation to a place we grew up in, or the university we attended, without needing to believe those to be superior to other places that we know less well.

Of course, some people do choose to change their countries. The not unfamiliar phenomenon of the migrant as civic patriot is particularly celebrated by those countries committed to an idea of citizenship and patriotism that is proactively open to incomers. It would be a curious logic that could accept migrant patriotism as potentially rational but that could not think of any reason why any of their fellow citizens might share it. Patriotism does not entail a 'my country right or wrong?' approach (or at least not necessarily so). The counter-point was pithily made by Carl Schurz, the nineteenth-century German revolutionary turned US Republican Senator for Missouri: 'My country, right or wrong; if right, to be *kept* right; and if wrong, to be *set* right.'

The patriotism of dissent can be a form of patriotism too. What is perhaps rarely noticed is how those who make appeals to national *shame* as an argument against patriotism are also paying an implicit tribute to national identity. However strongly opposed any of us might be to Russia's invasion of Ukraine, it feels less possible to be *ashamed* of it without being Russian. However much one may strive for the impossible task of consistently giving one's attention to every conflict and cause of wrongdoing in the world, almost all of us in reality feel more involved and implicated in the actions and choices of the countries of which we are citizens. Internationalists need to engage with national identity, since it is always being contested between various more inward- and outward-looking varieties. Countries such as Canada and Norway that are keen to do more in the world than might be expected of countries of their size do not just commit to meeting development aid targets first, or hosting

Middle East peace summits, or accepting refugees, only as citizens of the world. A commitment to internationalism can reflect a sense of what we believe we want our own country to be known for or to stand for too.

Yet it is common to hear the argument that patriotism seems to be an unnecessary and pointless distraction in times like these. It is an instinct that may be strengthened, particularly among those who think of their politics as progressive, when the economy is in a state, the least well-off are suffering most, and the planet is burning. This partly reflects a fear that the form of patriotism that would win out will be a new opium of the masses, distorting reality and distracting people from their real interests through a process of false consciousness. It is partly an instinct that this is all just a waste of time when everything else seems to matter so much more. But while it may be becoming more prevalent, I think this argument significantly underestimates the potential importance of patriotism in fostering precisely the sense of solidarity that can underpin and sustain effective social coalitions to tackle those priorities. It was a sense of mutual obligation and a duty of care for each other that created and sustained consent for welfare states and public services. Climate change will require global cooperation, it will depend on a sense of obligation towards each other at a local and national level too. Writing off patriotism as a distraction is a significant risk for those who have not yet identified a strong social glue to replicate it as a source of solidarity that can encourage us to pursue a common good.

Why flags matter: what sport taught me about identity

'All that I know most surely about morality and obligations I owe to football,' said the great French existential philosopher Albert Camus, who played in goal as a young man.[2] Much of what I know about national identity and patriotism, I owe to sport. This is partly because I was mainly just a sports-obsessed teenager, trying to keep my eye on the ball, when questions of identity kept butting in.

One reason I find it difficult to accept the critique that national identity is particularly irrational is that I am a football fan. If I had to choose the most irrational of my meaningful identities, I would surely have to say 'Evertonian'. This is a life-long allegiance that I certainly acquired by chance. Being part of this footballing tribe taught me many different things about how identity works, and the importance of making our tribes inclusive, both club and country.

I did not inherit any footballing loyalties from my cricket-mad dad. We were living on the Wirral, in Ellesmere Port, Cheshire and, if I was going to be a short, mixed-race kid in possession of a Scouse accent, I think my mum must have thought it would be a good idea to know a little bit about football. When I was five, she brought two football mugs – one with the Everton club badge, and the other with the Liverpool crest. I chose the Everton one and my younger brother got the Liverpool one. So I became a Blue and he was a Red. I really got the football bug, being incredibly excited to get the full kit (shirt, shorts and socks) when I was six, for Christmas.

I fully embraced the irrationality of my footballing tribe too. I was seven when my best friend told me that his dad said Evertonians should support Real Madrid against Liverpool in the European Cup final, so I did. My primary-school self was probably somewhat naive about the issues of 1980s terrace culture, but after an incessant three-year badgering campaign to attend a real match, that finally happened for my tenth birthday. At 12, I had a season ticket, watching the Champions of England, as they won the league title two years out of three (though, sadly, never again in the 36 years after 1987). This was an era when fans celebrated Merseyside's pride in the friendly nature of their rivalry. Ours was one of many cars to travel down to Wembley with one blue and one red scarf hanging out of each window on the motorway. Yet I was also tribal enough to refuse, on principle, to ever wear any red item of clothing, until I was 15.

My football tribalism suddenly changed one day – teaching me something new about identity. That day had begun as a fairly typical Saturday in my football-mad teenage years. The only unusual thing was that I was not going to a football match, but I had been playing football in the park with my friends before going home to listen to the football on the radio. I was more focused on Everton playing Norwich in the FA Cup semi-final at Villa Park than the glamorous tie between Liverpool and Nottingham Forest, taking place in Sheffield, at Hillsborough. The Everton commentary was interspersed with confused reports from an abandoned match. Switching on the TV, there were ambulances on the pitch. It was the day that 96 people who went out to a football match never came home. I doubt any news event will ever shake me so strongly. Most football fans in that era could recall experiences where that could have been us.

I am surprised, looking back, by how quickly many of us carried on. I was back standing on a football terrace the very next Saturday, as Everton visited Tottenham, in the eeriest atmosphere. Tears flowed during the pre-match silence, and exchanges of wreaths and flowers, before a subdued game of football in the April sunshine. It seemed a numb, collective act of bearing witness. The next weekend, I was at Wembley to watch Everton playing Brian Clough's Nottingham Forest in the Simod Cup final (a competition set up after English clubs were banned from competing in Europe following the 1985 Heysel disaster). Both sets of fans had Hillsborough on their minds. Yet as the teams exchanged goal after goal in an end-to-end match, their focus was already much more back on the game.

Liverpool did take three weeks off, to attend dozens of supporters funerals. Their first game was to replay that abandoned semi-final. As I tuned in to the BBC, something strange happened. For the first time in my life, I wanted Liverpool to win a football match, so they could play Everton at Wembley in the FA Cup final. (They did – and they won.) My new footballing non-tribalism had its limits: I was thrilled when Arsenal's dramatic injury-time goal clinched the league title at Anfield – as later immortalised in Nick Hornby's *Fever Pitch* – preventing Liverpool from doing the Double.

So the Hillsborough tragedy had not just changed how I thought about Liverpool, and football, but had given me a new understanding about how identity works too. Like most Evertonians, I was proud of how we mourned alongside our local rivals. Because this fierce and friendly rivalry was such a central part of what made us who we were, that made *their* grief *our* grief too. The tribal allegiance to our footballing colours would remain, but we understood better what we shared with the neighbouring tribe. I no longer tried to remain cold to 'You'll Never Walk Alone'. As I matured over the years, that transformative experience of Hillsborough could have become a useful pretext for going a bit too soft on our local rivals (though no self-respecting blue-nose should publicly own up to a secret crush on Jürgen Klopp, an awkwardly brilliant exemplar – the migrant as civic patriot – of the approach to identity and belonging that I want to champion).

Not everybody in my Evertonian tribe wanted me to be part of it. 'Everton are white' was one of the Goodison Park chants once Liverpool signed England's John Barnes in 1987. I am not sure how far I had clocked that my Evertonian heroes were still an all-white team back then. (After all, no team had any Asian players at all; something that has been slow to change since.) But the image of John Barnes back-heeling a banana off the pitch at

Goodison Park became iconic. So it was football that introduced me to overt, public racism at scale – and so to anti-racism campaigning too.

That my Evertonian tribe had a racism problem became impossible to ignore. It was pretty rare for that racism to be directed at me personally. I do recall hearing a voice, a few yards behind me, objecting to my blue and white tracksuit outside Crystal Palace's ground, saying 'even the Pakis are supporting Everton now'. I was on my own surrounded by West Ham fans, having secured a ticket in the wrong end of the ground for an FA Cup quarter-final in 1991, when they launched into singing 'I'd rather be a Paki than a Scouse.' Taken literally, this probably meant that I was safe, but I wasn't sure it was progress. I kept my Everton top well hidden.

We had moved to Essex so I was watching many Everton away games in the south, with trips to Merseyside too, while adopting a second team, Southend United, who often played under flood-lights on a Friday night. Overt racism was much rarer at Roots Hall. Having black players helped. I heard an incident of monkey chanting at a Wolves player directly challenged by another fan. 'Oi, mate, what's Andy Ansah going to think about that?' Essex may not be a heartland of liberal metropolitanism, but one of our early 1990s' chants was 'Ansah's black, Angell's white, we are f-ing dynamite.' The racism at Goodison Park receded sharply after the 1994 World Cup. Active campaigns from fan's groups, the launch of Kick It Out, our first black centre-forward in Nigeria's star striker Daniel Amokachi, a commitment from stewards and the police to eject and ban the racists, all helped to shift the culture.

I still did not know much about politics yet, except that I was starting to notice that politicians seemed unable to leave ques-tions of sport and national identity alone. I was 16 when Norman Tebbit, a leading voice in Thatcher's governing Conservative

Party, declared that too many British Asians failed his cricket test. 'Which side do they cheer for? It's an interesting test. Are you still harking back to where you came from or where you are?' he asked, curiously using an interview in the *Los Angeles Times* to offer his cricketing metaphor.[3]

My biggest problem with the Tebbit test was that I passed it. I can still recall today how dementedly my dad jumped around the living room as the seemingly invincible West Indies lost the 1983 World Cup final to India, who were then unlikely underdogs, nothing like the cricketing superpower they became later. I was happy that they won – but that was because India was his team, rather than being mine too. This Tebbit test didn't seem like cricket to me. Dad had been here for over two decades, working for the NHS. Expecting him to ditch India for England to prove his loyalty to this country seemed neither realistic nor fair. Dad, though, could find some particularly spectacular ways of failing Tebbit's test. I was a bit surprised, during the epic 2005 Ashes series, to find that he was supporting Ricky Ponting's Australia. I wasn't sure how far we should welcome his support for England when we played Pakistan.

There are many more considered arguments to be made about the Tebbit test, particularly about how we might best invite affiliation without insisting on it. Mostly, at the time, I just found the test divisive, rude and deeply irritating, for trying to turn what had been my natural sporting allegiance into some kind of political statement. It was too late to change sides now, so I just carried on supporting England at cricket (except, to be honest, when they played that brilliant West Indies team led by Viv Richards) but rather more quietly. Insistent demands for complete assimilation can set back the thing that they claim to want.

England, my England

After Hillsborough, I had got involved with fan-led efforts to shift the terrace culture. My student self had a green goalies' jersey with 'Camus 1' on the back and his quote about football and morality on the front. Maybe I was over-thinking the beautiful game, but the t-shirt makers at Philosophy Football had a much more grounded project than that when it came to how fans could try to reshape the stadium culture, and our national identity too.

I was among the voluntary group that put on fans' festivals at the South Bank ahead of Euro '96 and the 1998 World Cup, the brainchild of the enormously imaginative Mark Perryman. One of my bits was a 'Soccerati Tea Party' where Tom Watts (Lofty from *Eastenders*), who had written a history of the Arsenal North Bank based on the oral testimony of fans, hosted football writers, who were told to bring their club mug and given Wagon Wheels for sustenance, as they put the game to rights. We took that project into the stadiums too.

This was a time when England fans were associated with the worst excesses of xenophobic nationalism, chanting 'If it wasn't for the English, you'd be Krauts' at anybody foreign. There could be a mixed, edgy atmosphere in the pubs around Wembley near England matches. There is no way I would have risked the hassle of trying to follow the national team to any away game in the years before Euro '96. Talk about the decent majority was probably always true, but the idiot minority was vocal enough to make any game likely to be a mixed experience. Even Euro '96 itself came only months after England's friendly international in Dublin was abandoned the previous autumn following a riot in which the far-right Combat-18 group played a central role.

Our grassroots counter-message was simple, inclusive and patriotic. During my twenties, I was on several occasions part of the volunteers for the 'Raise the Flag' initiative at England matches. We put out red and white cards to make up a giant St George's Cross – with an inclusive message about England, and respect for the opposing team and fans too. (So, for example, we would also lay out a flag, in their colours, with our welcoming message in Swedish or German.) It was a pretty good deal: a free ticket for the England match, as long as you turned up several hours early to put the cards out before the stadium was open, and volunteered another hour at the end to pick them up. So the great cultural shift of Euro '96 and the fever of 'Football's Coming Home' – when England could play a positive role as tournament and festival hosts – were worked for by many fans from below. I was still in the ground, picking up our patriotic litter, after the last game at the old Wembley in 2001, where Germany beat England in the rain, when I heard that Kevin Keegan had resigned as England manager, bringing one cycle to a close.

England is a country of evolution not revolution, but the re-founding of England's football identity in 1996 involved the types of changes that are associated with new nation-states. That summer, we changed the flags to the Cross of St George – Union Jacks had flown around Wembley for the World Cup final in 1966 – and adopted a new (unofficial) national anthem of 'Three Lions'.

'Three Lions' rewrote the narrative. Telling the story of England from the fans' perspective showed that the old charge of post-imperial arrogance – that the country that invented the game had never come to terms with losing to foreigners – had long ceased to be true. England did not *expect* victory any more. We just remained committed to hope over experience. 'Three Lions' is a civic anthem that captures what it means to be a nation. The shared moments we experience together, of victory or agonising defeat, turn into not just personal memories but shared stories, new legends about who we are, which underpin our hopes and dreams for the future.

I felt much more confident about England and being English after that summer. The diversity of an inclusive Englishness was more aspirational than actual. It would be another generation before the diversity of the crowd gradually started to catch up with the idea. But it really mattered, to those of us who had experienced the previous 1980s' culture, that the ethos was much more of invitation than suspicion, hostility or exclusion.

A quarter of a century later, last summer, I had come full circle. It was now my ten-year-old daughter Indira who was watching live international football for the first time. Having filled in a wall chart at home for Euro 2020, we became quite loyal followers of England's Lionesses the following summer. Our fish and chips tour of southern England took us to watch group matches in both Brighton and Southampton, visiting the fan park to try out face-painting, table football and even a VAR simulator, seeking to get young girls and boys to aspire to be a referee. When England got to the final, our family group had the vantage point of the gods, seated in the top row of the top tier at Wembley stadium to see the Lionesses make history as European Champions against Germany. The crowds – just over half female, with lots of young families – represented as excitable and inclusive an English patriotism as anybody could imagine.

Despite the Lionesses' inspiration, the England men's team did not return from Qatar with the World Cup. It was a strange tournament, played at the wrong time of year, in the wrong place, for the wrong reasons. The muted reaction to England's quarter-final defeat by France (the team had played well, missed a penalty, and lost narrowly to the world champions) lacked the anxiety and anger of some previous World Cup inquests. Gareth

Southgate considered resigning but responded to the broad consensus that he should stay. It was disappointing to not get to meet the impressive underdogs Morocco in a World Cup semi-final, but the youth of England's talented young team, including 19-year-old Jude Bellingham, meant that there were high hopes for the future. At home, we had played 'Three Lions' for inspiration (both the 1996 original and the Qatar Christmas version for inspiration at half-time) and we sang it quietly while walking the dogs after the final whistle and the disappointment of the missed penalty. An England victory in 2026 – three decades after Euro '96 marked the thirtieth anniversary of the 1966 World Cup – seems almost written in the stars. Sixty years of hurt, for the men's team, certainly couldn't stop us dreaming.

So what had I learnt about identity from sport?

'The imagined community of millions seems more real as a team of 11 named people. The individual, even the one who only cheers, becomes a symbol of his nation himself', wrote Eric Hobsbawm.[4] We should neither underestimate nor overestimate how important sport can be in shaping national identity.

Sport often provides the focal point for the public conversation about national identity because (along with major royal occasions) it provides some of the few focal points where fifteen or twenty million of us still pay attention to the same thing at the same time.

Sport may be more important still because it provides many people with their first impression, at primary-school age, of what national identity is, and whether they feel invited to be part of it or not.

We should not underestimate sport because it does drive broader social change in how we talk and think about national identity. The athletes and footballers of the 1970s and 1980s did help to change who people thought of as British – and by the turn of the century as Scottish, Welsh and English too. Only 3 per cent of people now think it is very important to be white to be truly British. That nine out of ten people now think that Englishness is not ethnically defined is especially a social change driven by our national teams. Having secured those foundations, England's young players in the 2020s began a new public argument, in taking the knee, about what it meant to them that, for all the progress that has been made, they receive an excessive share of the racism that remains today.

I always found it a bit irritating when people on the left talked about 'reclaiming' flags from the National Front, the BNP and the EDL. I could not see why progressives were so keen to inadvertently concede the ownership of national symbols to far-right extremists, who thought they did own them but invariably lost their deposit whenever troubling the voters by standing for election. It certainly felt a bit retro that some were still talking about 'reclaiming the flag' at the 2012 Olympics, as if we hadn't done that back in 1984 and again in 1992.

Team GB in 2012 represented a confident and inclusive idea of Britain: a third of the medals were won by those born abroad, or who were the children or grandchildren of migrants. Having a multi-ethnic Team GB in the Olympics, or diverse groups representing England and Wales, Scotland and Northern Ireland at football, rugby or cricket, does not in itself make a national identity that is inclusive, but it can powerfully project an ideal about who we are now, an aspiration that most people believe in.

To align the aspiration and the reality, those moments need sustained work, within sport itself, and beyond it. Where sport has shaped a positive patriotism, it has done so with an attractive offer of an inclusive and shared identity. A more powerful example still than the remaking of football Englishness has been the

'Green and White Army' campaign in Northern Ireland, which took the challenge of a fan culture in which sectarianism festered, and did not just sanction or remove it, but replaced it with a positive fan culture that now dominates home stadium. It is a compelling contrast to the routine display of official UEFA anti-racism messages, paraded dutifully by players ahead of Champions League matches. *Don't be racist* is obviously a basic foundation – but that is a call to inaction. What we need is the positive emotionally powerful call to be part of the shared and inclusive tribe that we can all join.

But we should not overestimate sport's impact either. Having an inclusive idea of Britain for the Olympics and getting 'footballing Englishness' right had less of an impact in other spheres than I might have anticipated. Sport had changed perceptions of who could be British or English, with British identity being that which underpins the citizenship of the state, and so which was strongly reinforced in politics, business and civic society. There was less confidence that the progress made in the stadium extended to what being English meant outside of those World Cup or European championship summers. It won't be enough if it proves to be something that happens in only one sphere of society. The inclusive patriotism that we need depends on showing how to foster it outside of the stadium too.

The rational case for patriotism
(and the dangers of making it too rational)

There is a rational case for patriotism. Most people still think so today – in most places, most of the time. Patriotism has become more important as it has become more difficult: the liberal, individualistic, diverse and fast-changing societies that Western democracies have become today makes it all the more necessary to put in the effort, and to succeed in finding a sense of belonging that can bridge our differences.

Much ink has been spilt over how to differentiate patriotisms and nationalisms, good and bad. In his recent book, *The Great Experiment*, on the challenges of making diverse democracies work, Yascha Mounk calls patriotism 'a half-wild beast', capable of wreaking havoc if the worst people stoke its most violent instincts. But he argues that if decent people succeed in 'domesticating' patriotism, 'it can be of tremendous use in allowing the citizens of modern states to care for one another's fate'.[5]

In societies like ours, we need a civic and inclusive patriotism that can bind people together from different places, backgrounds, faiths and ethnicities, across social classes. Yet Mounk is right to warn that to focus on a civic patriotism of shared ideals and aspirations – often focusing on the constitution, in countries that have written theirs down – is incomplete and insufficient. The lofty ideals of an excessively civic constitutional patriotism do not fully describe what it is that citizens in diverse democracies actually love about their countries and share with each other. It is, I think, an underappreciated risk that the quest for an inclusive, inoculative and tamed patriotism becomes excessively rational – when it needlessly concedes all of the emotional content that it might want to make use of.

'Blood and soil' nationalism describes the most utterly toxic forms of expansionist and genocidal projects, from Hitler's holocaust to Pol Pot's killing fields in Cambodia. It is also a dead metaphor, a cliché used without thinking through the words. Civic and cultural patriotisms cannot be based on blood – but soil is not blood. An inclusive and civic patriotism should have plenty to say about place, rural or urban, and from coast to coast, about the land that we share now and that we all call home. An appeal to a shared sense of place can be one of the most important ways to at least manage and mitigate, if not necessarily transcend, some of the deepest social conflicts. It is because we live side by side that, whatever political choices are made, people across Scotland and Northern Ireland, Wales and England need to find ways that we can live well together.

What I would advocate is a new shared vision of civic and cultural patriotism – of story and song, of the places we cherish, of the land and the island we all call home – that is as confident about making an inclusive emotional appeal to the heart as well as the head.

That does not mean definitions do not matter. It is important for governments to be clear about the obligations of a common citizenship, particularly because the rights we enjoy depend on our willingness to respect those of others. So lists of British values can serve a functional purpose. Ofsted wants schools to know that they are founded on 'democracy, the rule of law, individual liberty, mutual respect and tolerance for those with different faiths and beliefs'. All modern liberal democracies are committed to broadly similar lists of values, but they have different histories and stories about how they got there, and make distinct choices, about the role of faith and whether the state recognises or avoids ethnicity, for example. Teaching citizenship in schools is all well and good, but what really determines whether or not we have an inclusive patriotism is whether students find what is taught on the curriculum more or less convincing, depending on their experiences of how this talk of a shared culture, of mutual respect, is lived and felt. Are we truly invited, on equal terms, both at those times when our country is coming together for major occasions, and more generally in our everyday lives?

So how we *experience* patriotism is much more important than how governments or political leaders make speeches or issue mission statements defining it. All of those arguments about whether or not we can 'define' a national identity have tended to underestimate the importance of each of us having 'lived experience' of national identity (perhaps different experiences, positive and negative) before we consider any political arguments or intellectual theories of ethnic nationalism or civic patriotism. My own experience of my national identities has been that we are talking about something meaningful and important, something that can be exclusive and inclusive, but above all something that can change and shift, if we want it to do so.

We do not all have to share exactly the same things. The clichés of our national identity are often broadly true generalisations for many people, but there is no obligation to like cricket, Shakespeare, Burns or Dylan Thomas, or even cups of tea, though queuing does represent a social norm on which other people will insist. The Coronation, the Eurovision Song Contest, the Olympics, and men's and women's football may each have distinct and overlapping audiences. Nothing is going to work for absolutely everyone. What matters is how far everybody feels invited to something that we can share. The most important way to be a patriot in a liberal and diverse society like this one is to work to make the inclusive patriotism that we do want to share feel real to as many people as possible.

A civic patriotism should have little fear of exceptionalism. There are dangers in chauvinistic or superior exceptionalisms – especially when combined with a sense of grievance and dispossession. But the truth is that all societies are exceptional from the inside. What makes a civic patriotism inclusive is not that it seeks to thin out our shared inheritance, but rather that it seeks to offer equal voice and status to those who join the club and to their children, so that the stories we tell about ourselves are open to challenge, across generations and across groups. One of the most important ways to do that is to understand the history of how we, the British, became us, the people we are today.

2

After Empire

The contested history of how we,
the British, became us

It was odd to realise that Enoch Powell's most fervent wish had been that I should never be born. For I did not yet exist when Powell looked ahead with such foreboding to Rivers of Blood in the most infamous British political speech of the twentieth century. It was only on the Monday following that speech that my dad got a plane from Delhi to London. Enoch's big mistake may have been to not secure stronger coverage of what he had to say in the Gujarati press. Dad came anyway and, eventually, he chose to stay. Though it would be another six years before I would be born, British, in a Doncaster hospital. Yet Rivers of Blood, at its core, had been a speech about me and, I should acknowledge, millions of others like me too.

Enoch's view of my birth was that it would be an all too avoidable tragedy. Powell noted that people sometimes pointed to the increasing proportion of 'immigrant offspring' born in this country as part of the solution. He could not have disagreed more.

The truth is the opposite. The West Indian or Asian does not, by being born in England, become an Englishman. In law, he becomes a United Kingdom citizen by birth; in fact, he is a West Indian or an Asian still. He will by the very nature of things have lost one country without gaining another, lost one nationality without acquiring a new one. Time is running against us and them.

Within a generation, Powell argues, we will have reproduced 'in England's green and pleasant land' what he calls 'the haunting tragedy of the United States'.[1]

Rivers of Blood is now recalled as a speech about whether politicians can talk about immigration or not. Yet Powell stated clearly that he saw stopping Commonwealth immigration as 'the minor part' of the issue at hand. With around half a million Commonwealth migrants already in Britain by the time my dad's plane landed at Heathrow. Powell was much more interested in the scale of repatriation – whether Dad and hundreds of thousands of others could be persuaded to return home. Mass repatriation would be voluntary, yet to be 'undertaken as a national duty ... on the scale which the urgency of the situation demands, preferably under a special Ministry for Repatriation' as he was to put it in his Eastbourne speech a few months later. Years later, Powell lamented that he had not left his quotation about rivers foaming in blood in the original Latin, suggesting that the nuances of his argument might then have been better understood. Almost everybody else in Britain got the gist, however, whichever side of these arguments they were on. It could be translated, at street level, into a simple, powerful, all too meaningful slogan: 'send them back'.

But it was not the Commonwealth migrants themselves who concerned Powell most. The truly existential threat would come from the birth, in Britain, of their children: people like me. My birth in a hospital in Doncaster was not an everyday story of celebration in NHS wards across the country. It is hard not to take Powell's declaration that 'it is like watching a nation busily engaged in heaping up its own funeral pyre' somewhat personally.[2] This metaphor cast each of us who were the children of Commonwealth migrants as just one more stick on this funeral pyre, just because there would be nowhere to send us back to. Powell's was a speech about my national identity – its sheer difficulty, its improbability and, in all likelihood, its ultimate impossibility. 'By the very nature of things', no less. The devastating consequence that would flow from this was the death of a nation, ending the possibility of patriotism itself.

Laughing at Enoch: how Powell lost the argument

Enoch was wrong. I have to argue that. He was wrong about the near impossibility of my ever feeling fully part of this country. That was part of a much bigger error. Enoch Powell represents the patriot as pessimist, but he was much too pessimistic about Britain. He was to define patriotism in 1977 as 'to have a nation to die for, and to be glad to die for, all the days of one's life'.[3] On that basis, Powell often said that he wished he had been killed, as he had expected to be, in the Second World War.[4] How odd, how nihilistic, it seems to me that so avowed a patriot could find so little confidence in the power of attraction that British identity and British culture could have for those who came to contribute to this country, or even for their children born and bred here, who might contribute to the next chapters of our long history.

It was Lenny Henry who dealt the knockout blow to Enoch Powell's argument. 'Enoch Powell wants to give us £1,000 to go home, but its only 20p on the bus to Dudley.'[5] What I love about that is its lack of fear. I have still never heard a better expression of the birthright confidence of the first British-born generation that we have an equal stake in this country. Our classmates too could see the sheer absurdity of somebody being unable to hear from Lenny Henry's Black Country accent that he was from *here* too. Yet this sense of standing was a significant shift between generations. Even half a century later, mentioning Enoch Powell's name to the first generation, who arrived around the time my dad did, will often evoke a visceral sense of how the mood shifted after that speech. Whether talk about 'keeping a suitcase packed, just in case' is intended literally or metaphorically, it speaks to a provisional and ultimately *revocable* status. It never felt like that to me at all. That was why Enoch could be mocked, rather than feared, by the 1980s and 1990s at least.

So what Enoch *had* been right about was the existential nature of that moment. My birth, and that of Lenny Henry, and two million others, had, simply by our being born, put his foundational objection to the idea – the reality – of a multi-ethnic Britain beyond realistic reach. Powell had seen this coming. He openly stated that he spoke with such fierce, unusual urgency in 1968 precisely because he saw this as a time-limited argument, to be acted on in that generation or lost for ever. He noted that it would be too late, by the mid-1980s, when half of the Commonwealth and Commonwealth-descended population would be British-born.

So Powell's core 'them and us' argument – that 'they' could never be 'us' – became a lost cause a very long time ago. By the time I would have first heard his name (as a teenager, in the 1980s) his foundational premise – that people like me could never truly share a country nor a national identity with most of the rest of you – was well on the way to being decisively rejected. The slogan 'Enoch was right' was fading into the past tense by then; a bitter and mildly coded lament from those who usually understood all too well that the moment for the argument had long passed. ('Enoch was right, of course, yet the sound take care never quite to specify what Enoch was right about', wrote Matthew Parris in his satirical lexicon of right-wing 'political soundness'.[6])

But settling one foundational argument can open up another. Commonwealth migrants and the children born in Britain were clearly here to stay. The future of Britain would be as a multi-ethnic society. But who do we think we are? If we want a shared British identity, do we need to agree on an account of our past to underpin that? We are certainly having *that* argument now – often with more intensity than a generation ago.

Time to forget about Empire: Enoch Powell's appeal to amnesia

I understood Enoch Powell better once he was dead. Grappling with identity issues meant I was definitely going to read Simon Heffer's 800-page *The Life of Enoch Powell* when it came out.[7] Though I do remember it might seem odd – even provocative – to be reading it on the train, or lazing around in the park. It is an indispensable book for understanding not just Powell but the making of modern Britain, given how foundational the argument he started about this was. It is a magisterial achievement in political biography because its author, who admired Powell, never shies away from any quotation that Powell's many critics would find useful.

That was how I found out, strangely, that India had played a more central part in Enoch Powell's sense of national identity than in my own. Powell's failure to persuade my dad not to come to Britain in 1968 was not the first time their fates had crossed. Enoch had himself been stationed in India when my dad was born there in 1944. 'I soaked up India like a sponge soaks up water,' he said. Young Enoch wrote home to his parents to declare that he felt 'quite as Indian as he did British' and – on the basis of his three-year posting in the country – even 'as Indian as any native'.[8] My jaw dropped. I would find it almost impossible to feel British 'by the very nature of things', remember. It was quite something to discover quite how much more fluidity Powell could grant to himself.

While Britain ruled India, there would be no more committed imperialist than Powell. His ambition to become Viceroy one day was his main motive for entering politics. He rejected entirely the growing consensus, with the Second World War ending, that Indian independence was now a matter of time. His 30,000-word memo, as a young party researcher, calling it 'a betrayal for which no legal or moral justification can be cited', was so strident that Churchill asked Rab Butler if he thought Powell was OK. The consequence of Powell's denial of what now seemed inevitable to everybody else was that he received the granting of independence as a deeply personal trauma. He later called it 'a shock so severe that I remember spending the whole of one night walking the streets of London trying to come to terms with it … occasionally I sat down in a doorway my head in my hands … One's whole world had been altered.' An earlier biographer, Humphry Berkeley, wrote that the loss of India was 'a spiritual amputation from which Powell has never recovered'.[9]

Powell responded to that shock by rewriting history. He reimagined his personal history, his political projects and the story of his nation. The most committed imperialist would now become the most fervent Little Englander of all. Powell's 1961 St George's Day lecture may never have become as well known as the Rivers of Blood speech. Yet it is equally revealing. I am not sure anybody else – left or right – has made a more audacious attempt to 'rewrite history' since.

Powell declares that the phase of Empire 'has so plainly ended, that even the generation born at its zenith, for whom the realisation is the hardest, no longer deceive themselves as to the fact'.[10] So Powell begins by making an argument *against* denial. But his case goes far beyond refocusing priorities to reflect new realities. Powell's post-imperial appeal is for England to forget – and to rediscover – an England to which Empire meant really nothing. He even inverts Kipling's famous lament to now suggest that 'perhaps, after all, we know most of England "who only England know"'.

> So the continuity of her existence was unbroken when the looser connections which had linked her with distant continents and strange races fell away. Thus our generation is one which comes home again from years of distant wandering. We discover affinities with earlier generations of English who felt no country but this to be their own ... who felt there was this deep this providential difference between our empire and those others, that the nationhood of the mother country remained unaltered through it all, almost unconscious of the strange, fantastic structure built around her – in modern parlance 'uninvolved'.[11]

Uninvolved! Could Powell truly believe these extraordinary intellectual contortions? That question may miss the point. Powell could sound surprisingly post-modern in arguing publicly that 'all history is myth', because 'the life of nations, no less than the life of men, is lived largely in the imagination'. 'The greatest task of the good statesman was to offer his people good myths, to save them from pernicious myths,' he argued.[12]

Powell's appeal to amnesia is a pernicious myth. His core purpose in it is to argue that, if the real England was 'uninvolved' in Empire, then the products of Empire should have no business in England. It is all the more pernicious since it was consciously made a whole generation after the UK government had issued a clear invitation to the Commonwealth and the colonies, stating precisely the opposite in the British Nationality Act of 1948.

We are here because you were there: a them and us narrative

'We are here because you were there.' That is the key response to Enoch Powell's appeal to amnesia, advocating that three centuries of British Empire should become a footnote for an unchanged England.

This aphorism to rebut that claim was coined by Ambalavaner Sivanandan, director of the Institute of Race Relations.[13] Though he had coined it a few years earlier, Sivanandan appears to have begun popularising the phrase around 1978. Margaret Thatcher, the leader of the opposition, had spoken empathetically about people's fears they might be 'rather swamped by people of a different culture'.

The aphorism is good history. It is undeniable, as a matter of historical sequencing, as a factual description of how one thing led to another. Post-war immigration was indeed 'part of the continuum of colonialism', as Ian Patel put it in his important study of immigration after Empire.[14] Though the invitation to come to Britain from 1948 did not arise because Empire was at an end, but because the British believed that it was not over. 'British Empire Gets New Nationality Act' was the *New York Times* headline about it. The Act defined British nationality by creating the status of 'Citizen of the United Kingdom and Colonies' (CUKC) as the sole national citizenship of the United Kingdom and all of its colonies. Conservative opposition spokesman David Maxwell Fyfe told the Commons that: 'We are proud that we impose no colour bar restrictions ... we must maintain our great metropolitan traditions of hospitality to everyone from every part of the empire.' Powell called it 'an evil statute'. In legislating for single citizenship across the United Kingdom and colonies, parliament's nationality law failed to define 'our own people'.

Narrowing citizenship was one argument that Powell did eventually win. His prescription of mass repatriation failed and faded. But the notion that politicians were unable to talk or act on immigration for decades is largely mythical. Though Ted Heath sacked Powell over the racialist overtones of Rivers of Blood, his government's 1971 Immigration Act ended Commonwealth free movement by 1973, while Margaret Thatcher's 1981 British Nationality Act followed through with a complex redefinition and removal of birthright citizenship. Of course, by then the multi-ethnic Britain that Powell feared was here to stay.

On what we remember and forget

The irony of Powell's appeal to amnesia is that it is now Enoch himself who is slipping away from public memory. I spent some time in the run-up to the fiftieth anniversary of his Rivers of Blood speech, talking to people in Wolverhampton, in Birmingham and in Dudley to find out how Powell and his legacy were seen now. I had gathered a mixed white, black and Asian group of people aged over 65. A couple of the group recognised their local MP. Not many could quite pin down who the West Midlands regional Mayor Andy Street was, though they knew they recognised him from somewhere. Our final picture was Enoch Powell in a Homburg hat. The group gave a laugh of recognition. They certainly knew who he was. And we were off into a compelling hour of the social history of Wolverhampton, the West Midlands and of Britain itself, as the group told us what he had said, why he had said it, how people had reacted at the time, and how attitudes had changed and why. Such vivid recollections: how a cross was burnt in protest at a Wolverhampton election count in the 1970s. We were even told which road Powell had lived on, and how West Indian nurses had moved into that road before the slightly more affluent adjacent street. The footballer Cyrille Regis had died a couple of days before we met. An older man talked about being taken by his father to see West Brom play as a teenager: how he had understood racism for the first time from seeing how the opposing supporters reacted to Regis and the trio of black West Brom players who had been nicknamed the 'three degrees'.

The following night, I was in the same place, talking to another group of local Wolverhampton residents, this time aged between 18 and 24. The photograph of Enoch Powell generated no recognition at all. 'Is he off *Peaky Blinders*?' somebody guessed. How about 'Enoch Powell'? The name meant nothing. Did 'Rivers of Blood' ring any bells? Nobody had heard anything about that either. Eventually, we explained the story of who Powell was and what he had said. The group had lots to say about migration, race and integration now – just without knowing that history. In a representative poll, under a quarter of ethnic minority respondents aged under 45 or their white British counterparts could match Powell's name to 'Rivers of Blood' though 90 per cent of those aged over 65 could do so.

Is forgetting about Enoch a good or bad thing? Many people care a great deal about history in Britain, but a common guilty secret is that we know much less about the history than we would like. If Enoch Powell is fading from memory, consider just how much more obscure most figures of the age of Empire would be. What do most people know about Empire? Next to nothing –

except that we had one, that it was big, that India and some of Africa were in it, and that it is over now. I doubt more than a handful of names from the age of Empire – beyond Gandhi, Queen Victoria and Churchill, maybe Cecil Rhodes too – are recognised by most people today.

This is an irony, too, of the 'history wars' that have broken out in the last few years. Few people outside Bristol had heard Edward Colston's name when his statue went into the harbour. In Bristol itself, Colston was ubiquitous. Girls from Colston Girls' School (renamed Montpelier High School in the aftermath of the drowned statue) used to go to the cathedral to mark his birthday, wearing chrysanthemums, his favourite flower. His statue was not erected until 170 years after his death. Its plaque declaring that the citizens of Bristol had erected this memorial to 'one of the most virtuous and wise sons of their city' was an artful piece of Victorian spin. Members of the Colston societies were reluctant to pay for the statue, but extending the appeal to the citizens of Bristol brought in nothing at all. By 2018, there was at least a consensus that the statue needed a new plaque, but there was a stand-off over what it should say. One draft was criticised for being too polemical against Colston; another for being too exculpatory.

Bristol is a liberal, affluent and rather segregated city. So years of arguments about Colston ran largely on parallel tracks. The case against Colston commanded a strong consensus at academic, literary and cultural events. Meanwhile, angry comments below the line on the *Bristol Post* website railed against those trying to erase the city's history. The city's business elites – once central to venerating Colston – tried to keep out of it.

Nobody seemed to create a forum where those views were likely to encounter each other, though this began to happen more after the statue was pulled down. Mayor Marvin Rees, among the first black mayors of a major city anywhere in Europe, made concerted efforts to reach across divides, with some success. A Bristol History Commission engaged in public consultation on a significant scale, with 14,000 people participating. There was a fair degree of public consensus on the statue being in a museum, with information explaining the events of June 2000. Colston Hall was finally renamed, with little controversy. The Society of Merchant Venturers, previously criticised as being 'the high priests of the Colston cult' by historian David Olusoga, played a conciliatory role too.[15] The day after the statue came down, they took no firm view about that, stating instead that it had long been divisive. 'Whether or not the city has a statue of a man known for his involvement in the Royal African Company, we must never forget the 12,000,000 enslaved human beings who were trafficked from their homes during the abhorrent transatlantic slave trade.'[16] It was perhaps not a coincidence that the venerable society had recently elected its first black British member in its four-century history. Long-overdue conversations were beginning in Bristol, in ways that could have lessons beyond the city too.

My campaign is for compromise on statues. I want to talk about which statues to put up. A polarising campaign to remove dozens of forgotten figures from their pedestals has little appeal to me. I would keep 99 per cent of the statues that we have got and try to shift the debate more towards who we should recognise rather than who we should remove.

The most egregious exceptions might go. If few people would keep up a statue of Gary Glitter or Jimmy Savile, it would be curious if no record of horrific evil from two centuries ago could be a disqualification either. I found arguments within Cardiff City Council to remove a statue of Thomas Picton – carried by 57 votes to 5 – convincing. Picton's conviction in 1806 as Governor of Trinidad for the unlawful torture of a 14-year-old girl had caused quite an outcry in his own time. Colston seems to me a distinct case from Queen Victoria, who was Empress of India, or Winston Churchill. Were Gladstone to be 'cancelled', could anyone from before 1900 hope to make the cut? What people were best known for in the past matters. We might cease to honour those whose central contribution to public life was wholly egregious. The stock of statues we inherit represents a layered account of what different generations and eras chose to value. The overall balance of choices reflects the values, biases and prejudices of the past. But it would be arrogant and flattening to now seem to put every statue on trial against contemporary mores. So 'retain and explain' – the shorthand of the approach preferred by the government – seems a good principle to me, most of the time. On one condition: that we do get on to the explaining. Yet the National Trust found itself at the centre of a noisy storm for doing precisely that, despite almost three-quarters of the public thinking that the Trust were doing the right thing, according to research carried out by the Policy Exchange think-tank.

In Edinburgh, Henry Dundas, 150 foot in the air on Edinburgh's Melville monument, is the subject of fierce controversy about the content of a new plaque (added in June 2020 following Black Lives Matter demonstrations) and the decisions he took two centuries ago.[17] The new plaque declares Dundas 'instrumental' in the delay to ending slavery, to be held responsible for half a million slaves crossing the Atlantic. Yet Sir Tom Devine has called this 'bad history', asserting that had Dundas not sought a delay, then 'forces political, economic and military were so potent that there was no way a British government would want to get abolition over the line'.[18] The new plaque, in flipping Dundas from hero to villain, arguably becomes a missed opportunity to educate about the slave trade: who supported it, and why, and how the balance of economics and politics shifted on that issue.

The rise of the *Windrush* narrative

'I did not want my children to grow up in a colony.' That was how *Windrush* passenger the late Sam King described to me his journey to Britain. Today, no account of the history of migration and the making of modern Britain could omit the *Windrush*. It was not, in fact, the first ship to arrive. The *Windrush*'s arrival in Tilbury in June 1948 coincided with the British Nationality Act's passage through parliament. So the ship was greeted with Pathé newsreel footage, which recorded calypso artist Lord Kitchener giving his first public rendition of 'London is the Place for Me', which he had written on the voyage. The *Evening Standard* sent a plane to greet the *Windrush*: its 'Welcome Home' headline emphasised just how many of these new arrivals were RAF servicemen returning to Britain.

Little was heard of the *Windrush* for four decades. There was a *Sunday Times* magazine profile of the Windrush generation on the twentieth anniversary, which came weeks after the infamous Rivers of Blood speech. But black Britain had little or no public voice, with the first post-war black and Asian MPs only entering the Commons in 1987. There were commemorations of the fortieth anniversary in Lambeth. It was the fiftieth anniversary of Windrush that took the ship's story from academic to mass public attention with a major BBC series and book by Mike and Trevor Phillips, establishing it as a key origins moment for post-war Britain, black Britain and Commonwealth migration. A cascade of cultural representations followed early in the new century, from Andrea Levy's seminal novel *Small Island* in 2004, later adapted for stage and television, through to the papier-mâché *Windrush* in Danny Boyle's Olympic opening ceremony, to the calypso classics in 2014's *Paddington* film, a story of migration and refuge, including 'London is the Place for Me'.

The Windrush scandal arose from the failure of governments to properly document the status of pre-1973 arrivals to Britain, combined with efforts in recent decades to create a hostile environment for those without legal status. But a lack of knowledge of the history of Commonwealth migration, race and Empire among officials and decision-makers was identified by Wendy Williams' 'Windrush Lessons Learned Review' as an important contributor to the injustices done to those whose status was simply not understood or recognised.

The National Windrush Memorial at Waterloo station arose directly from the government's apology for the scandal. This seventy-fifth anniversary year should be a story of pride as well as prejudice, a chance to reflect on the contribution and shifting experiences across three or four generations in Britain and to counter a fear of ever-increasing polarisation around the history of race and Empire by showing how we can talk about our past, present and future in which all of the stories can be told. Reflecting on three-quarters of a century of modern Britain should be a foundation, too, to start a new conversation about where we want to go next: to imagine the Britain we would hope to share by the Windrush centenary year, and to catalyse commitments to the efforts that could fully unlock that generational shift by 2048.

How to talk about Empire: beyond them and us

When we talk about the past, I think we now need to move beyond 'we are here because you were there'. This should be a first-generation dialogue – to explain the story of arrival. To remain stuck with it in a third or fourth generation would suggest we remain stuck in a 'them and us' dynamic. If it is good history, its logic as a normative argument is fuzzier. Do the wrongs of Empire generate rights? Is post-war migration a post-imperial form of reparation, even retribution?

It is indisputable that ethnic minority Britons are the product of Empire. Does that make us essentially its victims? Perceptions and experiences will differ. The sense that it still does is put potently by Akala in his book *Natives: Race and Class in the Ruins of Empire*,[19] particularly when he writes that 'even at five years old, we already know on some level that, in this society at least, we are indeed lesser citizens with all the baggage of racialised history following us ghost-like about our days. We are conquered people living in the conquerors' land, and as such we are people without honour.'

It does not feel like that to me, and that seems to be an argument that is difficult to sustain without acknowledging that we may sometimes feature among the beneficiaries of this era of post-Empire too. Not in full measure, compared to our white British peers, while structural disadvantage and discrimination exist, but increasingly so as they are diminished. 'I would be a dollar a day farmer if I was in Pakistan,' Conservative Cabinet minister Sajid Javid told me in a public event ahead of his 2019 bid to become the party leader. If few of us will reach that level, most ethnic minority Britons do not feel that we are 'people without honour'. Indeed, studies consistently find that the ethnic minority British consistently have a slightly higher level of attachment to British identity than the white British. There are some nuanced reasons behind that finding. It is partly about staking a claim to an identity that was challenged. The old National Front chant 'There Ain't No Black in the Union Jack' was repurposed by the academic Paul Gilroy as a title for his influential classic on race in Britain, first published in 1987. The cover image of a black veteran, war medals on his chest, signified how little the National Front knew of the history it claimed to be part of. The text explored how ideas of race and nation were

deeply interwoven. Early in the new century, in a strikingly optimistic introduction to a second edition, Gilroy wrote of how
British popular culture had put plenty of black in the Union Jack
across the 1990s.

Imagine that there was an enormous, imaginary red button. If
you pushed it, the British Empire would never have existed.
Would you, should you, push it? How could you not? Yet I have
to confess that I could not do it. However ignoble and selfish it
may seem, I would feel disinclined to write myself out of existence, now matter how much hypothetical suffering I might save.

But maybe others would be tempted to press that button.
Being willing to sacrifice me could allow the white liberal
conscience to emerge with cleaner historical hands. But then
think about who else might be keenest to press a button that
would make today's Britain considerably less diverse. Maybe that
would generate more mixed feelings too?

As an undergraduate, I could have spent weeks interrogating
this thought experiment from various utilitarian, deontological
and Rawlsian perspectives, making this choice behind a veil of
ignorance, where we would not yet know our own nationality or
ethnic group. Yet my counter-proposal would be that we should
not spend too long agonising over this hypothetical dilemma. I
am never going to be offered a chance to press that imaginary
button. Nor are any of you either. And that could be the foundational clue as for how we could get started on the conversations
about Empire and post-Empire that we need.

None of us can change the past now. None of us are directly
responsible for it. But take care before declaring that nothing
that happened before we were born can have anything to do with
us, as that might abolish the very idea of a nation. (If you have
no link to Empire, because you were not born, you could not be
proud of Shakespeare either.) We are all products of the Empire
and part of post-imperial Britain too. You do not need to have

parents from India or Ireland for that to be true for you. It may be more immediately apparent if you happen to have lived in Bristol or Glasgow, Liverpool or Belfast, Birmingham or London, but it applies pretty much everywhere across Britain once you start to think about it.

What we share now is a responsibility for how we choose to live with our past today. What do we forget and what do we try to remember? What do we want new generations to be taught about it? How do we relate to others who were involved, both at home and overseas? That is how we will decide how far the story we tell ourselves is open to hearing and telling all of our stories about how we got here – and the journey of modern Britain.

We are here because we were there. That is the story of how we, the British, became the us that we now need to explore together. If this can become something we can think about as our shared history, we would strengthen our sense that we can have a shared identity and a shared future too.

3

How Do People Become Us?

The patriotic guide to how we can make immigration and integration work fairly for us all

'There are too many of them.'

'They are taking our stuff.'

'They are not like us – and they don't want to be.'

'And we're not even allowed to talk about it – or they call us racist.'[1]

The most vocal arguments *against* immigration are invariably a story about 'them' and 'us'.

It is an argument that has recurred over time, and around the world, though in different times and places the case against 'them' will target different groups. Donald Trump might target Mexicans and Muslims. Viktor Orbán in Hungary is today the most vocal advocate of the Powellite argument that immigration will destroy the meaning of being a nation. In Britain, this 'them and us' case has been an argument about and against the Jews, and the East Europeans, and the Irish, and Commonwealth migrants from the Caribbean, or from India and Pakistan, or, later, European migrants from Poland or Romania, or hypothetical future arrivals from Turkey, or about the number of Muslims in the country, or the overall combination of 'other' groups who might one day, in some decades' time, in combination, lead to the white British being a minority in their own country.

The potency of this 'them and us' case against immigration comes from how it works at different levels.

It usually starts with an argument about numbers. Numbers arguments can be made about the total inflow of immigrants, or about the number of ethnic minorities in the population as a whole these days, or it might target a specific group. Whoever we are talking about in particular, the argument is about there being 'too many', too much and too fast.

Numbers matter because they open up an argument about resources – about who gets jobs and houses, or the overall risk that a small island is too full to let more people come in.

But arguments about the fair allocation of resources become considerably more powerful when they are combined with stories about identity and culture: that they don't like us, that they don't want to be like us. These are stories about who we are (and who they are not); about the history of how we got here (and what they would not understand about us), and what that clash might mean for us in the future.

And so that argument about resources and identity sets up an argument – and a grievance – about what all of this might mean for our democracy, about whose claims will be heard and recognised, and whose may be ignored and overlooked.

Yet this appeal to democracy sets up an important shift in who 'they' are. Because this 'them and us' story is not just about 'them' – the migrant and minority groups who may be coming in, and having this discomforting effect. There is another 'them and us' argument, because 'they' are also the elites; the decision-makers and the opinion formers in government and politics, business and the media. So the 'them and us' argument may decreasingly focus on its traditional target – the incomers – and instead direct its fire at the 'liberal elites' who will not recognise or do what 'the people' want.

Preaching to the converted on immigration

This 'them and us' case may shift form, but it is an argument against immigration that recurs down the ages. Many of the intuitive responses that come first to the liberal mind struggle to counter it – often tending to reinforce the populist case with those it is targeting, even if they resonate fairly well for those who were already immune from that argument.

So could those who want to defend the contribution of immigration to our society counter this argument in a way that is both authentic and effective?

One thing that won't work is trying to avoid the argument. It is easy to understand the temptation to do so, when this 'them and us' case is put in its most vocal, ferocious form. If the debate sounds too ugly, we might prefer to change the subject. Yet avoidance simply means the debate is being kept off limits to fester.

Another way to engage is to challenge the whole frame, and argue that, as our global connections grow, we should leave the whole idea of 'them' and 'us' behind. Why not, instead, think of ourselves as citizens of the world, including advancing the idea of a borderless world wherever we can. Naturally, this riposte will resonate most strongly with those who feel repelled by both the tone and content of the 'them and us' case. The obvious problem arises, though, of how to make that case resonate beyond those who instinctively hated the 'them and us' argument. A response to claims that 'they' will be bad for 'us', which questions whether there is really any need or sense in trying to maintain a sense of 'us' any more, may serve to confirm rather than refute the argument.

A pragmatic alternative is to contest the evidence, seeking to refute the detailed claims made for the 'them and us' case, by addressing the grievance that migrants take resources that should be ours. Much pro-migration advocacy takes this form, with the main argument being about the *net gains of immigration* – that *immigrants contribute more than they take out*. The focus is often on the economic benefits of migration, a case often made by employers and business voices, and commentators in outlets like *The Economist* or the *Financial Times*. Parallel arguments about the cultural gains of diversity are made by civic voices, commentators and politicians. These arguments will be familiar. 'We have had a long history of immigration. Migrants don't take out: doesn't the Treasury data show a net fiscal contribution to the public purse? There are benefits of cultural diversity: we could surely all agree migration improved our food.' These liberal homilies may capture important parts of the whole story. But such arguments will resonate most with those who have no need to be convinced or reassured.

Those making an evidence-based case are seeking to appeal to pragmatism, implicitly shifting the balance of the argument from values to interests. The reason that this pro-evidence case struggles to persuade is not really in the contested details of how strong or weak such evidence might be on specific questions, though there is, paradoxically, strong evidence from political psychology and brain science that evidence-based arguments turn out to be a much less effective way to make the case for migration than those pursuing it instinctively feel it will be. This could be called the myth of myth-busting.

The underlying weakness of the appeal to think rationally, weigh up the pros and cons, and understand that 'they' are good for 'us' is its transactional nature. What can be overlooked is that the contention 'they are good for us' – while clearly much more benign in its intention than the 'them versus us' polemics – is itself another kind of 'them' and 'us' argument. But 'they are good for us' is a much narrower and more limited case than one where we approach immigration and integration in a way that expands, over time, who we think the 'greater us' can be.

Why 'they are good for us' is not enough

The 'them and us' debates about the pros and cons of immigration easily get polarised and stuck. They are largely exercises in talking past each other. An argument of mutual incomprehension between those who would embrace and speed up change, or slow it down, between those who see greater openness as widening the circle of compassion, and those who fear that other voices get left out and left behind. David Goodhart has described this as the clash between the 'anywheres' and the 'somewheres', the global and the local, arguing for a rebalancing back from the cosmopolitan to the communitarian.

We could get further in bridging these divides if we thought about how the patriotic case for managing immigration and promoting integration can break down the 'them' and 'us' divide. The argument here would not be that we don't need an 'us' any more in an increasingly global world, but rather one that accepts that identity may matter more, rather than less, in fast-changing and polarising times. What we should be striving for is the broader story of the bigger 'us' – shared local and national stories about what we have in common.

This would be an argument that accepts that fairness means thinking about how to treat people who come to a new society fairly – and what fairness means for the communities they join.

It would see this not just as a question concerning the fair allocation of resources, but about having a bridging approach to identity too. I am not arguing that the patriotic case for immigration would or should be the only case for immigration. Not all of my liberal friends and allies want to make it so. Of course, those who want to make an 'open borders' case for global cosmopolitanism can do so (if they want to) but, personally, I am sceptical about it. In a liberal democracy, migration policies will become more open when there is sustained political and public consent. Where there is confidence in the historic handling of migration, and the contemporary experience of integration, there will be permission for future migration. Where that is not the case, there will be pressure to at least slow down the pace of change. Parliaments and voters can decide to remove borders – as those countries that are part of the European Union have done between themselves – but that will depend on securing and sustaining sufficient democratic consent to be part of that club.

There is no obligation on all of those who favour immigration to make the case in ways that have a better chance of persuading others, if that comes at the cost of the integrity of their own argument. But seeking to give a greater share of voice to this patriotic case for migration and integration could be one of the most likely routes to break through what can seem to be a polarised deadlock.

Can we imagine a shared future in polarised times?

The founding of the think-tank British Future in 2012 arose out of thinking strategically about what would need to change if the case for immigration and integration – that Britain could be a more confident, more welcoming and more inclusive country –

could be made more effectively to sceptical audiences, rather than simply preaching to the converted.

That meant taking seriously the different types of reasons that people have for being sceptical, especially the doubts that mattered to engageable sceptics, who were not diehard opponents of migration or ethnic diversity.

First, this meant that an effective case for immigration depended on being willing to open up public debate rather than to close it down. If people do not feel they can have a voice on a major issue, that is corrosive. While the argument that the immigration debate is kept off limits contains a large dose of mythology (when the statute books are full of mostly restrictive legislation, passed in each of the last seven decades) it is also clearly a fear that has resonated. It needs to be addressed by a sustained, visible effort to ensure that people do have a voice, which ensures that a full range of voices can be heard, and which then has a stronger foundation for drawing the line against prejudice.

Second, it meant understanding that how people think about immigration is about more than immigration. Immigration is partly a debate about policy – who gets to come to our country; the rules and systems that admit them. But when we talk about immigration, we find ourselves talking about many other things too, beyond who gets a visa or why, or what happens at our borders. We need to consider how we think about the pace of change, the impacts on our economy, on jobs and housing, and on culture and integration too. This is part of a much broader argument about economic and cultural confidence: what we think has changed for the better or for the worse. Will there be fair chances for my children? Will Britain still be Britain – and what is it that we share today?

Third, and most crucially, these questions about immigration, integration and identity in Britain today have never been questions that migrants and the children of migrants could navigate alone. The choice of the name British Future for the think-tank reflected these two principal insights. 'British' because these are ultimately questions for everybody in our society, not just for those joining it, where the answers would depend on what we think is fair, and on who we think we are. 'Future' because we need to understand how we got here, but to also ask where we are going.

There are different experiences, frustrations and grievances about the past – about what governments have got wrong and about which voices have not been heard. The key to a more constructive conversation and agenda is to accept that we do start from here, and so engage people in the question of what we should do now. That is a practical question: about how we identify the constructive ways to manage issues of migration, integration and identity fairly, both for those who come into our society and for the communities they join. It is a question of vision and identity too. Ultimately, the most important way to bridge a 'them and us' polarisation on immigration and identity would be to develop a conversation about the common ground – about the future that we would want to share.

Why are people changing their minds about immigration?

The last decade has been among the most dramatic in the history of immigration to Britain. It has also been a decade of two halves in public attitudes. The EU referendum showed that governments had lost public confidence in relation to the scale and pace of immigration. Yet five years after the vote to leave the European Union, Britain had become much more relaxed about such immigration. These were the biggest ever shifts in attitudes towards it in Britain, and as significant a shift on this issue as can be found in modern times in any major democracy. The Brexit vote was the crescendo of two decades of immigration scepticism, making a significant and probably crucial contribution to the outcome, yet it increasingly now also looks like a high-water mark as a longer-term generational sea-change is counter-intuitively catalysed and reinforced by Brexit itself.

The proportion of people wanting to reduce immigration – invariably two-thirds of people in recent decades – fell below half of the population for the first time. There was still a significant divide over immigration numbers: around four out of ten people still wanted to see overall immigration fall, and one in four wanted to see large reductions, while half of the population were now content to see high immigration levels continue, including a quarter who said they wanted to see overall immigration increase. Among those with the most liberal views, this combined with a sense of regret at the end of free movement; those most in favour of immigration tended to be the only group who thought that migration, overall, had fallen after Brexit.

Why did attitudes change? It is a nuanced story, because different people changed their minds for different reasons. There were long-term gradual shifts in view; from rising graduate education; from the growth in meaningful contact arising in the long run from migration and diversity; and from gradual shifts in views across generations. But there was also a significant acceleration of change immediately after the 2016 referendum.[2]

Catharsis played a crucial role. The argument that it was impossible to talk about immigration had never been less credible. Immigration had been central to the public debate about Britain in Europe. The majority vote to leave had, eventually, led to the biggest changes in the immigration rules for four decades. Free movement from the EU ending, replaced by a new points-based system for work visas, treating European and non-European migration similarly. Whatever the pros and cons of these changes, they were proof that immigration politics and policy could change in response to public voice.

This did not resolve the contested argument about immigration and racism. The argument over how much of the Brexit debate was driven by prejudice became more polarised. But nobody could claim that the political system was keeping immigration off limits and refusing to talk about it at all.

Control was an important part of this story. Those who were open to immigration, but wanted to be more selective about who came in and why, got what they wanted. But control changed the immigration debate in another crucial way. More control meant more responsibility for the choices that were made, and this directly led to a broad public awareness that these were complex and nuanced questions. The choice to be made was no longer one of for immigration or against it, or being for or against free movement, nor even the overall question of whether or not to try to reduce the numbers. Control meant a dozen different choices – what to do about students; and doctors and nurses; and bankers and lawyers; and those coming to work in care homes, or restaurants or to pick fruit? Control highlighted that people think rather differently about different kinds of immigration. Most people who wanted control turned out to be selective and pragmatic about when to use it.

Government policy would be in favour of 'the brightest and the best', accepting immigration for high-skilled and high-paid jobs, though Boris Johnson's government softened Theresa May's initial policy and made visas available for more mid-skilled jobs via the points system. The public were relaxed about that kind of immigration, but did not take such a binary view of the policy. Letting bankers come in and pay taxes had brought pragmatic support, but more visas for social care workers was somewhat more popular. Naming jobs increased support for immigration significantly. Many of those in favour of reduced migration, overall, did not want to apply that to many specific examples at all and there was growing support for increased migration of doctors, nurses and care workers, as well as a dramatic spike in support for letting more fruit-pickers come to Britain.

A growing public awareness of the positive contribution that immigration can make was as significant as control. In a long-term tracker of immigration attitudes, conducted by Ipsos-Mori, those respondents whose views had become more positive were asked what they thought had made a difference. 'I am more aware of the positive contribution of immigration now' was a typical response, deemed to be more important than having greater control.

Stories are more important than statistics, whether those statistics are negative or positive, relating to the pressures of population growth, or to the economic contribution to GDP. One thing that happened, several times over the decade, was that statistics took on voices and faces. The million Polish migrants in Britain, among the three to four million European nationals, were now people who were anxious about securing their permission to stay in Britain. In the week after the referendum, 86 per cent of people wanted government to guarantee their rights immediately. It was not an issue that split the Remain-voting 48 per cent from the Leave-voting 52 per cent but rather common ground across the two tribes.

There was a dramatic surge in support for taking refugees in response to the tragedy of three-year-old Syrian refugee Alan Kurdi, who drowned when the dinghy he had crowded on to with his family capsized off the Turkish coast, a short distance into their attempt to reach Greece. For many people, their response to the tragedy was connected to their experience of being a parent.

While just about everybody is against 'illegal immigration', the Windrush scandal showed the human cost of applying the rules unfairly, including to those whose legal status was not recognised. It showed too, as Wendy Williams' report set out, that the 'institutional thoughtlessness' about racial discrimination was not simply a feature of policy-making in the 1960s.

Immigration for the NHS was already the front-of-mind example of the benefits of immigration, but the Covid pandemic had a dramatic impact on perceptions. A decade ago, the public thought that, on balance, immigration brought more pressures than gains to the NHS. That flipped dramatically, with a net increase of 42 per cent in those seeing immigration as positive for the NHS between 2012 and 2022. The trade-off between two competing intuitions – the potential pressure of a rising population, and the contribution of NHS workers – shifted decisively.

So 'imagined immigration changed'.[3] It was not just that we were thinking more about different archetypes of immigration. It was that we were more often aware of the human dimension of immigration. There was considerably less about immigration, in the aggregate, on the front pages of newspapers. The coverage had become more positive.

Migrants and refugees have done extraordinary things – creating Marks & Spencer's, the Paralympic Games. Sometimes, fairy tales do come true. The fact that a refugee might invent the next Google is not an especially persuasive case for refugee protection. Indeed, what is more likely to build confidence in migration and integration is not so much the extraordinary stories as the normal ones – the refugee children who get good GCSEs and go to university, the parents who get a job as a car mechanic or teaching assistant while giving their children a new start in life. It is those everyday stories of contact that are more likely to shift the norm.

And yet it did matter that one of Britain's most extraordinary migrants had a much more incredible and haunting story than anyone had imagined. Sir Mo Farah revealed in a BBC documentary that he had been trafficked to Britain as a nine-year-old, forced to work as a domestic servant, before being rescued by the intervention of a PE teacher, Alan Watkins. His real name was Hussein Abdi Kahin, rather than Mo Farah. Reading between the lines of Farah's 2013 memoir *Twin Ambitions* it seemed clear that Watkins had done something to regularise his status when he was first picked for England juniors. What I found most striking was how Farah's reaction to the news – that the Home Office regarded his case as in the past – was one of relief. Mo Farah's choice to tell his story put a very famous face to the story of trafficking. Obviously, people react to that story now through knowing who Mo Farah is and his place in national folklore. But that emotional reaction to the story is not just about his winning four Olympic medals. Before all of that, he is a nine-year-old and then a twelve-year-old boy with a life to lead – and thanks to the support of the school, and then the government of the day, he gets to lead his life. He does extraordinary things with his opportunity, but humanising the story gives us an empathy with the idea that any young boy has a life to lead.

That is another indicator that control matters. Dangerous journeys across the Channel are nobody's idea of a safe or effective system for claiming asylum. Most people feel some sympathy for those making perilous crossings, combined with concern at the visible lack of control.

Pitting control against compassion generates a stalemate on asylum. A third of the public are attracted by tough messages to deter; a third think it is unconscionable to consider any such thing. A large chunk of the public do not want to be forced to choose between control and compassion because they believe that a competent government could have both. The government relished the chance to battle in court with bishops, lawyers and refugee NGOs to show it was tough on asylum, but it may have misread the shifting public mood. Its Rwanda plan is a performative headline-grabbing policy, which distracts energy, time and large amounts of money (Rwanda received £120 million, 0.5 per cent of its GDP, for a policy that is unlikely to ever happen at any scale) from pursuing the multilateral cooperation and domestic asylum system reforms needed to design an asylum system that is orderly, effective and humane.

How do people become us? The patriotic case for citizenship and integration

How do people become us? That is the key question in this age of identity. This is not just a key to sustained public consent for immigration. I believe that those societies that are more confident about patriotism in the next half-century will be those that feel most confident about how people become us.

The first point is simple: you have to decide to be a country that wants new people to become us, believing this to be both desirable and possible, rather than one that does not. And while equal opportunity is an important part of feeling invited to be fully part of a society, a sense of equal status and belonging is at least as important. This is something that societies can choose to do something about, particularly in the decisions they make about citizenship.

That is not simply a matter of clear processes and policies concerning how to become a citizen, and transparency about the rules and expectations. It is just as importantly about whether those who become citizens in law do feel that they are invited to become 'us' – fully, equally part of who we are, emotionally in spirit. That is a reciprocal relationship. It is about how migrants themselves feel about the terms on which they are accepted, but it is also about how everyone else feels about that too.

Different societies have had different intuitions about this. Japan is the OECD country historically closest to the closed end of the spectrum of a civic national identity. Societies where an ethnic conception of identity dominates may be open to temporary migration – if visiting guests can make a useful contribution, whether in high-status roles in finance and academia, or in low-paid work, often with precarious rights – but will be unlikely to encourage incomers to become citizens. Japan has remained pretty allergic to immigration for settlement, whatever the demographic arguments in favour. No other advanced democracy makes a weaker contribution to refugee protection, Japan having granted refugee status to just 21 people in 2018 and to 42 in 2019, from 11,000 asylum applications – an acceptance rate of 1 per cent.[4]

Germany was the biggest convert from a primarily ethnic to a civic conception of national identity and citizenship. This was the lesson of the unintended consequence of the *gastarbeiter* (guest-worker) model. The German post-war model tried to balance two messages: that Germany needed and welcomed guest-workers, and that they should always remember they would be going home again. So 'Germany is not a county of migration' became a policy mantra, even as fifteen million guest-workers were invited to the country. Remarkably, the government even organised televised ceremonies for the millionth and two millionth guest-workers to come to Germany (these presented them with flowers, or a television set) while emphasising that that welcome was temporary.[5] So the German model was consciously *anti*-integration; it actively promoted segregated schools, because migrants were not expected to become German, nor invited to do so, though some Turkish parents did fight to have their children admitted to mainstream schools. The long-run dilemma of the guest-worker model was summed up in Max Frisch's famous aphorism: 'We wanted workers – but we got people.'[6] A major national debate in the late 1990s gave rise to the Federal Republic's new citizenship laws which came into force on 1 January 2000. After its long history of ambivalence, Germany has a good claim to be the liberal democracy that puts most proactive resource into migrant integration today.[7]

What vision of integration should we pursue? For me, integration is about inclusion, being fully part of our society – feeling 'integral' to it. Integration is a broadly popular idea across minority and majority groups, despite the history of anxiety within the liberal left as to whether the idea of integration sounds too assimilationist. Curiously, this concern seems to have become stronger in academic and civic society circles, in a liberal era when there is considerably less pressure to fully assimilate. Today, particularly in large and diverse cities such as London and Manchester, Bristol, Cardiff and Glasgow, there is clearly a great deal of autonomy and support for maintaining and blending heritage and identities. For Jewish migrants in the 1890s and 1920s, and Commonwealth migrants in the 1950s and 1960s, and the British-born children of these groups, the pressures of navigating the challenges of identity were probably much sharper than they are today.

There are different dimensions to feeling integral to a society. There are the tangible socio-economic facts about the presence or absence of equal opportunity. How far do migrants or their children have fair chances, and no unfair barriers, in education, in applying for jobs, in progression in whatever field they choose? But feeling integral depends on something more subjective, but equally important: equality of status.

Do people like me have an equal stake and claim, and do other people treat us as having so? This *reciprocal* relationship is crucial for equal status. There is no point deciding that I want to identify with my country if it mostly rejects the identity and allegiance of people like me. So civic and legal rights need to be reflected in social norms and public attitudes. That question of identity may be just as important as socio-economic outcome.

A 'full integration in one generation' test could be one of the best barometers to show how far a society lives up to the ideal of integration in practice. That would be informed by the tangible socio-economic facts, of outcomes in education, employment and progression. Yet it may depend above all else on perceptions of belonging.

One sign that a society is getting this right is if you do not hear much talk about 'second- (and even third-) generation immigrants' in politics, the media and civic society discourse. The style guide of *The Economist* magazine makes this core point well: 'Generations. Beware. If you are a second generation immigrant, it means you have left the country that your parents migrated to.'[8] (My brother, British-born but now a naturalised Canadian dual citizen, is happy to use the term in this literal sense.) Any society that talks routinely about 'second-generation migrants' and especially one where the idea of a 'third-generation migrant' makes sense is conveying that the children, and even the grandchildren, of migrants are often still perceived more as 'them' than 'us', an indicator of a persistent gap between the legal facts of equal citizenship and the social perceptions of what that really means.

There is a third key to getting integration right. We cannot do it unless we know the answer to the question: 'integration into what?' We need to know who 'we' are if we want incomers to join our club. With a confident sense of ourselves, others adopting that shared identity becomes a vote of confidence in that tradition, not a dilution or threat.

Britain has many of the ingredients to get this right – perhaps as strong an opportunity as anybody else. What we have never yet done is act proactively to achieve this. If those who choose to become British exemplify the civic idea of a 'new us', we should encourage people to become citizens and celebrate it when they do.

It is too easy to be snarky about the citizenship test – a good idea, which should be better executed. Too much of the citizenship test reads like a civil service entrance examination paper – how many days a year do schools need to open by law? Its core flaw is that seven out of ten existing citizens do not pass it if they have not swotted up on the handbook first. Yet getting the citizenship test right is easily fixed. Panels of the great and good have pored over the handbook. The public – both British-born citizens and those who have become British over the decades – could help to apply the obvious common-sense test: are we asking our new fellow citizens to learn things that the rest of us know?

When British Future brought British-born and new citizens together in Southampton and in Edinburgh to talk about the citizenship process, we tried some of the test together. Those born in this country were baffled by the level of historical knowledge involved. Yet new Britons spoke up for history as a theme of the citizenship test, saying that knowing a country's history helped to understand the people, and should be included alongside the practical information. And some British-born participants, unsure of the point of citizenship ceremonies, found themselves persuaded by new citizens that these felt important – a celebratory moment after a long journey to becoming British.

There are practical barriers to Britishness. The cost of British citizenship is the highest in the Western world. Remarkably, if one could go on some kind of 'supermarket sweep' to acquire citizenship in the USA, Canada, Australia and France all at once, the combined cost would add up to less than the £1,330 cost per applicant in the UK, which is almost four times as much as the cost to the Home Office of processing an application. That leaves a family of four with a bill of almost £6,000, before legal fees. It is because government has been entirely agnostic about whether people become British or not that it has created unnecessary cost and process hurdles. If we want to welcome people becoming British, then the citizenship process should not be so complicated that most people cannot apply without a lawyer. The government should conduct a review of citizenship policy; its aims and objectives, the processes, systems and costs, and how to do things better.

Citizenship forges common bonds between new citizens and the society they have joined. It helps if that is visible. If we welcome it when people decide to become us, we should invite those settling in our society to become British, and celebrate it when they do. An annual high-profile national citizenship ceremony hosted by the King and the Prime Minister, at the Palace, perhaps coinciding with special events in iconic locations, from Edinburgh Castle to York Minster, Stonehenge to Cardiff's Millennium Stadium, led by devolved governments, local councils and institutions keen to be part of this welcoming effort.

Perhaps the best test of all of an inclusive patriotism is how to be the country that is most confident about how people can become us – not just in law, but in spirit too. Why don't we choose to be the country that puts most effort and energy into celebrating those who join our society and who choose to become British?

4

Reinventing Our Traditions

Why we need a bridging monarchy to strengthen the ties that bind

King Charles III may turn out to be a lucky king. He has certainly inherited a monarchy in much more robust condition, a couple of decades into the twenty-first century, than either he or almost anybody else expected.

The King may be relieved to consider how much more stable his accession has been than he might have feared when the Queen had declared 1992 to be her *annus horribilis*, as the announcement of Charles's separation from Diana coincided with the Windsor Castle fire. After the outpouring of public grief for Diana after the great shock of her tragic early death, each gradual step in the relationship of Charles and Camilla was gingerly handled with much caution and care, right up to the Queen stating, on the eve of the Platinum Jubilee in 2022, that Camilla becoming Queen Consort would be her own personal wish. There has been hardly a murmur of public contention or controversy concerning the crowning of Camilla as Queen alongside Charles as King.

For a long time, many of Britain's republicans had attributed a good deal of the extraordinarily stable support for the monarchy to the presence of the Queen, predicting that her heirs and successors would struggle to transfer and maintain that sense of public allegiance. Perhaps, in the long run, it may turn out that way one day. What happened, however, in the autumn of 2022 was that the proportion of people who thought that Charles would make 'a good king' doubled overnight, from 31 per cent to 62 per cent, bringing his personal reputation broadly into line with support for the institution itself. There is a certain logic in those who support the institution of a hereditary constitutional monarchy aligning their view of the institution with the individual who has become its figurehead.

So, the lesson of this very stable transition is that the republican perspective tended to significantly underestimate how much more of the burden of proof lies on those proposing a change to set out why the gains would outweigh the cons. This year of royal ritual, in both mourning and celebration, has projected the case for continuity quite strongly. The sense that nowhere else does tradition quite like the British has been a recurring theme. We do need shared rituals, shared experiences and national moments to share a society. Over the past generation, many people have worried about whether our individualistic liberal societies of almost infinite choice, for all of the freedoms that we value, may leave us with too few shared moments and institutions that connect us. So it makes sense to ensure that we use those that we already have. That is why I have changed my own mind about the monarchy.

What may be most distinctive about Britain is not just our pride in tradition but our ability to change. A bridging monarchy could provide one of the great 'show not tell' champions of what an inclusive patriotism could mean in practice. The monarchy's distinctive ability to provide a bridge between traditional and modern Britain could allow the King to gently reinvent the institution to play a more proactive civic role in polarised times.

I think it could also exemplify a broader rule on how to bring Britain back together, that may have the most impact in helping people to reconnect, not by inventing new traditions, but by renewing and reinventing old traditions for our times.

Reinventing the monarchy: lessons from history

'The British persuaded themselves that they were good at cere-monial because they always had been',[1] historian David Cannadine noted about the increasing popular power of royal ritual in the first half of the twentieth century from 1918 to 1953 – an insight that can now be updated to the 2020s.

This sense of timelessness can make the continuity of such rituals and traditions seem like some kind of conjuring trick. Given the pace of social, cultural and technological change over the last seven decades, both supporters and critics of the institution may wonder if the institution of monarchy can really maintain this suspension of gravity and somehow survive in the internet age.

Yet this sense of timelessness is also something of a historical mirage. Royal traditions certainly do stretch back over a thousand years in one form and another. The first Coronation in England, that of King Athelstan, took place in September 925. King Charles III can also claim a direct link through James VI (James I of England) and Robert II of Scotland to a thousand years of Scottish kingship, going back to King Kenneth MacAlpin.

Yet the long history is much more complex and contested than this imagined sense of timeless tradition conveys. Indeed, Cannadine's authoritative study of royal ritual characterises the period from 1820 to the 1870s as one of 'ineptly performed ritual' with little public reach or appeal, in stark contrast to the confidence, splendour and reach of the monarchy's heyday in the century and a half since. 'For the first three-quarters of the nineteenth century, Royals were almost without exception viewed with indifference or hostility', Cannadine writes.

King Charles III is only the thirteenth British monarch since the Act of Union. And taking this longer view generates a surprising insight. The King probably inherits a stronger hand at the time of his Coronation than almost all of his dozen predecessors of the last three centuries, with the sole exception of his own mother Queen Elizabeth II. The height of British republicanism came as Victoria largely ceased to perform the public role of a constitutional monarch in the 1860s after Albert's death. The monarchy did recover significantly after her return to public life in the 1870s, so that both the 1897 Diamond Jubilee and her funeral projected the power and prestige of Britain in the imperial age. That high era of the invention of royal traditions would have been rather more difficult without the participation of the monarch herself. The accessions of the early twentieth century – taking place during the constitutional crisis of 1910, shortly after the revolution in Russia in 1918, and in the wake of the abdication of 1936, meant that the monarchy felt somewhat more fragile and contingent in those accession years than at the beginning of this reign. The 1953 Coronation took place shortly after the Second World War, the twin legacies of which were to ratify a sense of confidence in British institutions, while also catalysing the key reforms of the modern post-war welfare settlement, to make this perhaps the peak moment of national and social cohesion, but considerably more the exception than the rule over the last three centuries.

Despite Bagehot's famous warning about the risks of 'letting daylight in upon magic',[2] each shift in media technology has helped to extend the reach of the modern monarchy; with newspaper photography in the nineteenth century, radio broadcasts of the 1930s, and television in 1953 giving an enormously greater public reach to royal ceremony than had been previously possible. Even our own era of much greater fragmentation offers opportunities to the monarchy, as comparable national focal points become rarer, while the internet amplifies its global reach and status further.

Why I changed my mind about the monarchy

'It is a strange fact, but it is unquestionably true that almost any English intellectual would be more ashamed of being caught standing to attention during "God Save the King" than of stealing from a poor box', George Orwell wrote in *The Lion and the Unicorn*.[3] That book was pretty much my favourite piece of writing, from the time I first read it, probably when I was around 18. But that bit could have been about me. Maybe I figured, back then, that with my Irish *and* Indian heritage, if I wasn't going to be pro-republic, then who on earth would? Not that my dad would have agreed.

I had once seen the case for a republic as common sense. Why should the highest role in the land be open only to those who were born to it? But I changed my mind gradually – becoming, across different phases, convinced by three different arguments in favour of the monarchy.

My first reason for retreating from republicanism arose from recognising how many people did not agree, so it seemed prudent to admit defeat. That became easier to do as I increasingly decided that the role of the constitutional monarchy mattered rather less than either its critics alleged or its supporters claimed. If Britain was more hierarchical, unequal or undemocratic than it should be, I became sceptical about how far removing a largely decorative constitutional monarchy was the key to changing that.

After the last polarising decade, I have changed my mind again. I would now place less emphasis on the harmlessness of monarchy in politics and more on its potential utility for society. The constitutional role is fixed, but its civic role can evolve. With increasing concern about what divides us, and what can bring us together, I think we should place a higher premium on the symbolic and the practical value of institutions that can play a part in helping to transcend our divides and provide moments and opportunities that can bring us together.

I now think there is a strong rational case for a constitutional monarchy. I can also feel the appeal of some of the less rational reasons to support it too, especially after I became a parent in my early thirties. The 2011 Royal Wedding of William and Kate was the first big royal event that our two eldest children, then five and three, were conscious of. As I took a photograph of them on the doorstep, decked out in paper crowns, heading to celebratory parties at primary school and nursery, it struck me just how much more liberating it might be on these national high days and holidays to stop worrying and to learn to love the monarchy. Even if I could sense that I might just have fallen for the most effective propagandist trick – get them young – that the Establishment could pull, I was struck also by how it seemed much too miserabilist to worry about that, rather than accepting the invitation to the party, and by how little I wanted to convey to them (not just yet anyway) that there might just be two sides to this argument. But maybe my republican friends would be cheered up to hear that my teenage children are swinging more towards their side of the argument. During the 2022 Jubilee celebrations, my 16-year-old daughter proposed that the best thing to do would be to quietly bring the monarchy to an end after the reign of the Queen, *but without hurting her feelings*. 'We wouldn't have to tell Lizzie that this is what is going to happen,' she suggested. She says she is still making her mind up about King Charles; she definitely felt it was 'too soon' to be singing 'God Save the King' when we saw the Lionesses play again at Wembley, only a fortnight after the Queen's funeral, especially given that we were watching the England women's team.

The democratic case for Britain's hereditary monarchy

The strongest argument in favour of a hereditary monarchy in modern Britain is a democratic one. That sounds like a paradox. 'The Queen is Dead! Long Live the King!' No campaign to elect the King on the death of his mother was necessary, because our system acclaims a new head of state, by automatic hereditary succession, at the moment of death.

Yet the core democratic principle underpinning the republican movement – why shouldn't we choose our own head of state for ourselves? – turns out to clash with itself. It would surely make public consent an unassailable condition of change, not just in practice, but in principle too. There is no barrier to Britain becoming a republic should most citizens want to make that change – a principle accepted from Barbados, Jamaica to Australia or Canada, and that surely applies to Britain too. Conversely, this means that should not happen for so long as the monarchy has broad, sustained public and political consent.

Around one in five citizens (19 per cent) supported a republic the first time there was a modern poll on the topic conducted by Mori in 1969. The level of support is almost exactly the same now, half a century later. Public opinion expert Bob Worcester has called it 'the most stable measure of public opinion that exists in this country'.[4] To put it another way, it could be fairly claimed that the campaign for a British republic has been perhaps the least successful political campaign of my lifetime. I feel republicans have tended to convey a disdain for supporters of a constitutional monarchy, casting them as unwitting dupes of media propaganda. Opposition to the hereditary method in principle is clearly legitimate, but do republicans acknowledge that there could be legitimate reasons to support it too?

The republican movement should acknowledge that Britain's constitutional monarchy is a democratically legitimate institution, until it can convince sufficient people of its case. But I think that its acceptance of this argument would depend on the *quid pro quo* of giving its supporters a fairer share of public voice. This did not happen during the mourning period for the Queen during the autumn of 2022. Broadcasters erred very strongly on the side of caution, respect and deference.

I did find the images and stories from 'the Queue' compelling, as a quarter of a million people turned a cherished national cliché into a tribute to the late monarch. Vanessa Nathakumaran, from Harrow via Sri Lanka, some decades ago, was the very first person to queue overnight. I admired her and all of those who stoically endured the 12-hour shuffle of this modern pilgrimage for a few moments of sublime silence in the presence of the Queen's coffin. We did not join the queue: my ten-year-old declared herself staunchly pro-monarchy (unlike her teenage siblings) but sensibly said she would have been willing to queue for up to three hours, but not longer than that.

Yet the queue did not represent the sentiment of all of Britain. Coverage accurately reflected broad goodwill for the new King, but could also exaggerate the scale of consensus, by suggesting that majority view was close to unanimous. The police had to be reminded that 'Not My King' is free speech. But disrespect is not disorder. The projection by national broadcasters of too much unity could fall short of how they should cover the contested arguments for a constitutional monarchy in our liberal democracy.

In principle, it would be possible to prove the democratic legitimacy of the monarchy in a hyper-rationalist way. For example, by scheduling a confirmatory referendum to coincide with the May local elections after the beginning of a new reign. I doubt there was any appetite in the Palace for running for re-election in the run-up to Coronation Day. There certainly doesn't seem to be any public appetite to do this – just 22 per cent of people wanted a referendum in a YouGov survey just after the accession – not least because we already know what the result would be. One reason that an actual referendum is unnecessary is because there is already a permanent metaphorical referendum. Even those who inherit their constitutional powers are subject to the tyranny of the opinion polls. King Charles III does not, perhaps, face what Bill Clinton in the White House once called 'the daily referendum', but from year to year, and decade to decade, maintaining sustained public consent is essential to the self-preservation of the institution.

The case against the monarchy that I had taken most seriously was that this symbol of hereditary privilege was important in preventing Britain from becoming more equal and more democratic – as a stifling symbol of hierarchy and social class, or an impediment to the democratic change and proper scrutiny of Executive power. So the second phase in my change of mind was in coming to think that the monarchy did not matter so much as either its critics or its advocates claimed. I came to doubt that the monarchy made much difference to the political and social outcomes in our society. This was how Orwell came to think of it. He hoped for an egalitarian social revolution in England, but imagined that it would be one that will 'not be doctrinaire, or even logical', leaving 'loose ends and anachronisms everywhere' – that it would abolish the House of Lords, but probably not the monarchy.

The monarchy had not prevented the creation of the NHS and the Beveridge welfare state by Clement Attlee, nor could it impede the rolling back of that post-war settlement by Margaret Thatcher, and the subsequent rise in inequality. Attlee had himself set out why 'the Labour party had never been Republican' in arguing that social progress has usually been stronger in limited monarchies than in republics.[5] Today, the pro-equality book *The Spirit Level* by Kate Pickett and Richard Wilkinson champions Sweden as the strongest example of actually existing egalitarianism. Whatever it may be that prevents Britain from emulating Sweden and choosing to be more equal, it seems unlikely to be the existence of a constitutional monarchy, given that Sweden has a king or queen too. Whatever their scope and limits, it is clear that the bigger constitutional choices, from joining the EEC in 1973 to Brexit in 2020, whether to abolish the Lords for an elected Senate, devolution, or even changes to the electoral system, are separate from the existence of a constitutional monarchy itself.

The appeal of the modern monarchy comes in large part from its retreat from political power, so that it is now above the political fray that it would once have been embroiled in. Powerlessness brings risks too. It is a curious aspect of the British constitution that one of the key principles of British public life is to protect the head of state from public controversy. The reserve powers of the monarch, for example, to dismiss a Prime Minister, do remain a final back-stop power in the British constitution. But the emphasis on the constitutional monarchy as a dignified, ceremonial, even primarily decorative part of the constitution could mean that constitutional norms could lack protection if these came under increased pressure, as Peter Hennessey has observed of the non-prorogation of 2019. 'A government proved willing to counsel the use of powers in a way that was controversial.'[6] This is not a case against having a constitutional monarchy in the role of final arbiter and referee, but for normalising the constitutional role and powers. That could help to demonstrate its civic purpose, promote some constructive reforms, and suggest alternative ideas too.

The bridging Crown: what should King Charles change?

If our modern sense of the timelessness of the monarchy was achieved by the invention and reinvention not just of royal ritual and tradition, but of its civic and social role, this offers a tradition of gradual modernisation that the new King could now renew to find a role in these times that would not just serve the institutional instinct for long-term self-preservation, so that the monarchy survives for the next half-century and beyond, but also plays a useful social role.

Charles had reportedly considered becoming King George VII, or Arthur or Philip, to avoid the historic omens of being King Charles III. Acceding at 73, it was probably sensible to maintain the name that the British public had known him by for decades. Beyond that first decision about his regal name, the big question facing the new King is how much to modernise a monarchy during and beyond this Coronation year. Having waited longer for the role than any previous heir, we wait to see whether he may have seen his modernising dissipate since the 1990s, or whether he might prove an old king in something of a hurry to make his mark. In his first broadcast as King, Charles took care to acknowledge that he now faces new constitutional constraints on his public voice, by stating that he would have less time for his causes and charities. His exhortation to William and Kate, now Prince and Princess of Wales, to lead national conversations that could 'help to bring the marginal to the centre ground where vital help can be given' showed an awareness of the value of the monarchy reaching out beyond its traditional core of support.

The King saw his personal reputation and levels of public approval rise, coming into line with support for the institution. As indicated earlier, there is a natural logic in supporters of a hereditary constitutional monarchy deciding to support the incumbent (or rethinking their support for the institution if they are unable to do so), compared to, say, a party leader or national football team manager, where a more imminent change might be possible. Expectations of what it is to be 'a Good King' may well be somewhat higher in terms of public service and commitment in the twenty-first century than in the eighteenth or nineteenth. Several of the King's predecessors may have struggled under modern scrutiny to keep the Crown.

To decide on how he might define that himself, the King will need a clear public narrative of what a modern monarchy is for. This kingdom is more anxious, fragmented and divided than we are used to or than any of us would want. The monarchy can be a public institution committed to defusing identity conflict, by promoting meaningful contact across our divides. How effective it will be in this will depend on how far the monarchy can itself bridge to its own more sceptical audiences. Support for keeping the monarchy is rock solid among older people in the south of England. The Jubilee Britain research published by British Future during the spring 2022 Jubilee found that only a minority of those in Scotland, of ethnic minority Britain, and of the youngest adults were actively in favour of the institution, with as many indifferent or on the fence as were in favour of a republic. So the Coronation vote of confidence in the monarchy comes with three challenges for the long-term health of the institution: securing support across the UK nations and regions, including in Scotland and Wales; reaching across the generations; and ensuring the Monarchy can maintain broad consent across different ethnic groups.

Why reinventing traditions can do more for bridging than inventing them

Of course, if we fear that collective experiences are becoming too scarce, we can try to do something about it. We would not have any traditions if somebody, sometime, had not invented something – perhaps sensing that there were identity gaps to fill. There is nothing to stop us inventing our own traditions. That means it will make sense to think about how we can make the best use of those that we already have.

That the Queen died in Balmoral placed Scotland at the centre of a United Kingdom-wide national moment. This gave the slender pro-UK majority in Scotland a sense of public visibility that many feel they have lacked since the 2014 referendum but it may well have done as much to reinforce existing views on all flanks as to change minds. Queen Elizabeth II was more outspoken, albeit in code, about the Union than about any other public issue, except the Commonwealth. Her Silver Jubilee speech of 1977 contained a somewhat balanced argument about understanding the aspirations for devolution, but its ending that 'I cannot forget that I was crowned Queen of the United Kingdom of Great Britain and Northern Ireland' conveyed a clear message. However, the Queen opened the Scottish and Welsh parliaments once they were legislated for, perhaps playing a significant role in helping to broaden the legitimacy of the Welsh Senedd in particular. While the Queen's 'think very carefully' intervention was ostensibly within the bounds of neutrality during the 2014 referendum, it was clearly briefed and reported as a partisan preference.

It is not the King's job to campaign for the Union. It is unclear that the King could or should do much proactively for the Union in Scotland, beyond providing a Show Not Tell symbol of the

United Kingdom that other campaigners can make something of. The King's role is not to represent 55 per cent of Scotland but to reach across the political divide over independence. It would make sense for Scotland's independence movement to pledge, as it did in 2014, that an independent Scotland would maintain the monarchy and join the Commonwealth, not simply to try to engage swing voters to reach 50 per cent of the vote, but because the achievement of independence would require an engagement with the British identity of a very large minority of Scots.

Why the monarchy needs to reconnect with Britain's minorities

That ethnic minority Britain is now more on the fence about the monarchy reflects a significant shift across the generations in black and Asian Britain. The first generation of Commonwealth migrants to Britain could see in the late Queen what we might in modern parlance call an 'ally' (albeit a symbolic and somewhat distant one) who at least knew and symbolised in her commitment to the Commonwealth, the history of Britain that too many other people did not know. My dad supported the monarchy. He associated Queen Elizabeth II much less with the fading story of the Empire into which both she and he had been born, and more as the most visible public champion of the post-imperial Commonwealth links that explained why he was British.

The late Queen had the right opponents anyway. What is mostly now forgotten is how Enoch Powell, having lost his argument for mass repatriation, launched an extraordinary attack on the monarch after her 1983 Christmas broadcast featured images of the Queen meeting Indira Gandhi on her trip to India for the Commonwealth heads of government meeting. Powell felt this would 'suggest she has the affairs and interests in other continents as much, or more, at heart than those of her own people', especially when 'even here, in the UK, she is more concerned for the susceptibilities & prejudices of a vociferous minority of newcomers than for the great mass of her subjects'. Powell saw this excessive royal empathy for Commonwealth citizens abroad and ethnic minorities in Britain as 'pregnant with peril for the future' of the monarchy, 'threatening the place of the Crown in the affections of the people'.[7] It was another pessimistic Powellite prophecy that was proved wrong.

In recent decades, the monarchy was much more engaged with the diversity of the Commonwealth abroad than with British diversity at home. It had an exemption from the race relations legislation. There was little ethnic diversity to be found anywhere in the British Establishment. That began to change, gradually, in the early years of this century. The honours lists saw efforts to reflect service and contribution. If being honoured in the name of a no longer existent Empire was a barrier for some, many others could still accept it, often talking about what that would mean for their parents and grandparents. But if the Windrush generation of Commonwealth migrants often saw the Crown as a symbol of the history that they felt more people in Britain should know about, that story feels considerably more distant to their British-born grandchildren.

The unhappy departure of Prince Harry and Meghan Markle exacerbates this generational challenge. That was, to say the least, a significant missed opportunity for a bridging monarchy. It was a fairy tale that quickly turned sour. Their wedding itself was a cause of significant celebration as a symbol of social change. At one level, this was rather overdone. Meghan Markle was never a British Obama. She had married a prince, not run for public office. Part of the initial fairy tale was that Harry and Meghan overcame the obstacles to their love match. There is a long tradition of Royals being impeded from pursuing the relationships they would have chosen for themselves. In falling for an American, a divorcee and a television actress, Harry crossed several red lines that courtiers in the 1950s or 1980s would have insisted upon, even before Meghan's mixed ethnic heritage came into the picture. Meghan's distressing personal account of the impact on her mental health, including revealing that she had suicidal thoughts, evokes echoes of the clash between a young Diana and the cold formality of institutional bureaucracy. The comparison weighs heavily on Prince Harry, who was just 12 when his mother died.

When my parents met in the late 1960s, the dominant critique of mixed-race relationships was that it would be selfish to foist the inevitable identity crisis on to the children. When Prince Harry was born in the 1980s, a majority of people had doubts about how they would react to their child marrying across ethnic lines, but attitudes changed as ethnically mixed relationships became less unusual. The marriage of Harry and Meghan did not need to transform social attitudes towards inter-racial relationships in Britain. Rather, it exemplified the social changes that had already taken place, but that also remain a work in progress.

After their departure from the royal family, Harry and Meghan became much more polarising figures than before. The scale of income received for giving their side of the story in both a Netflix series and the Prince's biography *Spare*, as the couple sought to establish their financial independence, appeared difficult to reconcile for many with concerns about privacy or hopes of a family reconciliation. There was limited public sympathy for the couple in Britain in the wake of their decision to depart. But the generational chasm in views at home appeared at least as signifi-cant as the transatlantic divide. Initially, the under-twenty-fours had been sympathetic to the departing couple by three to one, while the over-sixty-fives were unsympathetic by six to one. Even the generation gap on Brexit was much narrower than this. One could have different views about why the young might see it differently – according to taste, reflecting greater empathy towards mental health, naivety about celebrity culture, or an indicator of 'wokeness' to be praised or deplored, but it will have reflected and reinforced a sense of greater indifference to the monarchy. That generational chasm shows why the monarchy has been resisting efforts (sometimes from those who think of themselves as its most vocal champions) to use the Royals as ammunition in the so-called 'culture wars', as a symbol of enduring tradition that can see off the emergence of 'woke' ideology. Rather, it needs to bridge the generational divides. While the monarchy chose, officially, to make no on-the-record comment in response to Prince Harry's book, it should have been possible to publicly express disapproval of the Jeremy Clarkson column in *The Sun* expressing hatred for Meghan Markle 'at a cellular level', given that it became the most complained-about article in the history of the press regulator Ipso, and was indeed withdrawn at the request of its author.

Yet, ultimately, it should never have been the job of one princess of mixed ethnic heritage, rather than the national institution itself, to engage with the diversity of modern Britain. The monarchy will need to work harder again to engage across the generations in an increasingly multi-ethnic society. Those continuing to increase the temperature will harm that effort.

The King's multiculturalist declaration of his 'duty to protect diversity' will enable him to use his Coronation to show how he intends to blend his responsibility as Head of the Church for Britain's Christian heritage with his commitment to our multi-faith present. A focus on multi-faith dialogue may well have more appeal to older than younger people. Reaching across the generations may involve a greater willingness to engage with the complexity and controversies of British history.

The monarchy is itself a product of a thousand years of immigration and integration; recasting its Norman, Dutch and German origins into the sturdy oak of the House of Windsor, it should be a natural champion of new Britons. The coincidence of this Coronation year with the seventy-fifth anniversary of the arrival of the *Windrush*, the symbolic origins moment of a postwar multi-ethnic Britain, offers the King an ideal opportunity to engage as significantly with Britain's diversity at home as it has with the Commonwealth abroad. On Windrush Day last year, while Prince William unveiled the new Windrush national memorial at Waterloo station, Charles, then Prince of Wales, announced that he had commissioned portraits of members of the Windrush generation to be put on show at Buckingham Palace as part of the Windrush anniversary celebrations. He said:

> The *Windrush* vessel arrived at Tilbury in the year I was born, inspiring a generation who made this country home. I have always thought of the United Kingdom as a community of communities whose strength is in our diversity and over the last 75 years this generation has made an immeasurable contribution to the society we share. That is why, in this special anniversary year, I wanted to pay my own heartfelt tribute to the role they have played in our nation's story.

This warm gesture of recognition also offers one foundation from which to consider how best to engage constructively with the sharper edges of the history of race, Empire and decolonisation.

Why reinventing traditions works better for Britain than inventing them

A bridging monarchy can play a key role in ratifying and projecting a modern British patriotism. The Coronation captures a national pride in the place of tradition and history in Britain. At the same time, when I think about what has changed over the half-century of my lifetime, I feel that we could make almost as strong a case that we can do change and openness pretty well too.

Political scientist Karen Stenner's research suggests that around one-third of the population across democratic societies have a tendency towards authoritarianism, which can be triggered by a sense of rapid change or a heightened sense of conflict. Yet even a symbolic focus on unity can reduce this perception of threat, and this can be combined with the substance of progress. The constitutional monarchy may therefore play an important role in both reassuring those concerned about the pace of change and including those anxious about their acceptance in British society.

It is useful to consider why the 2012 London Olympics opening ceremony succeeded where the Millennium Dome failed just over a decade earlier. The Dome was part of a conscious act of national 'rebranding'. This meant that it was in many ways envisaged as a story that Britain (or its government) wanted to project to the wider world, about a young and modern Britain. The origins of the project were cross-party, yet the message became associated primarily with New Labour's political project. The Dome left a tangible local legacy in North Greenwich, but as an effort at a new national narrative, it was largely an iconic failure. In a bid to be inclusive of some of those previously excluded, and trying to be everything for everyone, it ended up being for no one. The underlying message – 'the future, not the past' – was too binary. Britain does not think of itself as a 'young country'.

Without being rooted in the story of how modern Britain got here, the message about modern Britain seemed rather unmoored and contentless. It did not attempt to bridge our past, present and future.

The Olympics saw Danny Boyle in 2012 succeed where the Dome failed. That night, twenty-seven million of us watched a compelling story about our past and present, in which modern Britain was shown to arise as a product of our long history – of the Industrial Revolution, war and Empire, cultural and techno-logical change – rather than being a modernising rupture from it. This was widely celebrated as a critical and public success.

There is no barrier to the invention of new traditions, but there may be a particular value in how the reinvention of existing ones may often prove most effective in bridging social divides.

Remembrance offers another strong example of the gradual reinvention of existing traditions. It is important that marking Remembrance Day has begun to significantly and proactively broaden its appeal across ethnic and faith minorities in recent years. It is seen as important to honour service and sacrifice: a not-well-known fact is that the armies that fought the two world wars resemble the Britain of the 2020s more than that of 1914 or 1940 in their ethnic and faith make-up. A significant rise, particularly during the First World War centenary, in public awareness of the scale of the Commonwealth contribution deep-ens the opportunity for Remembrance to become an annual moment of bridging social contact, and to begin to better reflect this message that everybody is invited to share in the local prac-tice of Remembrance. It is an inherently bridging message, supported by three-quarters of the ethnic minority and ethnic majority groups, because it combines a message of overdue recog-nition to minority groups, and a message of perhaps surprising reassurance to some older white British conservative voices that these traditions matter in a diverse Britain.

It is not the role of a constitutional monarchy to be in the vanguard of change. That would be to usurp the role of other political, civic or business actors. It can help to ratify those social changes that have happened, and help to make new connections that can unlock their potential for the common good. If the Queen symbolised stability, just by always being there for all of our lives, the King can be a more proactive bridger. The new civic role of a bridging monarchy may be to proactively celebrate and project an inclusive patriotism in which Britain does not choose between tradition and change, but seeks to knit them together into something we can share.

5

Hate

The fear and loathing of a changing Britain

I could not help but think about Stephen Lawrence just about every day in 1999.

We were the same age. Stephen had been born British too, in the Greenwich District Hospital in September 1974. Yet his life had been cut brutally short one April night when he was just shy of 19. Stephen was killed, because of the colour of his skin, as he waited for the number 161 bus that would get him home from Eltham to Plumstead.

I found myself living on Eltham's Well Hall Road, where the murder had taken place, as the public inquiry saw this story of injustice dominate the national news headlines. Not even ten yards from our house, there was a simple plaque in his memory, next to the tree where Stephen, having tried to run and escape, had fallen and died.

We had only been living in Eltham a handful of weeks – and this was now some six years after his murder – when the public inquiry set out the lessons of the long saga in which the police had failed to bring his killers to justice.

There was fresh embarrassment in February 1999 for the local police too. White paint was splashed across Stephen's memorial on the day of the report's publication. It was a gesture of racist disrespect. It turned out that the surveillance camera overlooking the memorial was simply a dummy, containing no tape, adding insult to injury, and one more unsolved crime to the catalogue.

So we acquired a permanent policeman, somewhat in the style of 10 Downing Street, deployed to keep careful watch over this scene for the next week. This piece of stable-door bolting prevented anything else untoward happening. But my wife Stacy did at least give our bored doorstep copper something to do by accidentally locking herself out of the house one morning. He resourcefully got her back in through the back door without a key, before radioing these live neighbourhood developments – 'cuppa at number 324' – to colleagues patrolling further up the road. As they gathered in our kitchen, the rank and file turned out to be not fully aligned with the Met Commissioner's talk of atoning for the past and learning the lessons so that things could be put right. The bobbies on the Well Hall Road beat did talk about their sympathy for the Lawrences as parents, but mainly expressed their open sense of grievance about the unfairness of the public kicking that the police were now taking from all quarters about this case.

Their feeling was that the police had become the scapegoats of the media, who were blowing this case up into something political. They had tried to solve this crime, like any other crime, yet the failure to convict in this case had been 'turned into a race thing too'. But who was really to say that this was what had gone wrong? There was a deep defensive discomfort with any idea that the police's failure to solve the case had anything to do with race. Any nuances intended by labelling this 'institutional' had made little difference there. Yet that sense of unfairness and grievance – even questioning whether other unsolved murders, say, of a young white teenager, would have got quite this level of attention – echoes the attitudes that the inquiry itself had identified as central to the initial failures of the investigation.

Our own presence on the Well Hall Road was largely a matter of chance, itself one tiny part of how the local area was gradually changing. Three years out of university, my first proper job had been working for a book publisher, whose academic division was in unglamorous Basingstoke. So Stacy and I had moved in together and bought a small end-terrace in nearby Winchester the previous year. Relocating for a job in London, we looked for something comparable around zone four. We were exchanging on a renovated terrace in gradually gentrifying Plumstead when the developer sold it to somebody else, so we were then shown a house a couple of miles away in Eltham. Though I certainly knew the Stephen Lawrence case from the national news, I had not absorbed its precise local geography. Nor was this a selling point that the estate agent sought to stress. So we only made the link to just how near this infamous murder had been shortly before exchanging contracts. After a few further enquiries, we decided to carry on.

Eltham was a pretty white area, certainly by south London standards, rather more so then than now, if compared to nearby Woolwich and Plumstead, though much the same could be said of posh Blackheath, also a couple of miles up the road. Most mornings at Eltham station, I could pick up a newspaper and read intrepid investigations about the fear, loathing and racism half a mile away on the Progress Estate: 'the truth about Eltham' and even 'Into Hell' as the headlines put it. Yet my Eltham was mostly the routine of the suburban daily commute. As I walked a few hundred yards from Eltham station home each day, it was impossible not to think about what had happened to Stephen as he looked frantically for the bus that might get him home to Plumstead. I will forever be bewildered at the contrast between that blur of hatred that saw Stephen killed in a few frenzied seconds, and the mundane normality of this busy suburban road, with its local Co-op, curry houses, kebab shops and newsagents, and the Coronet cinema, a grand, fading grade-II-listed 1930s art deco affair, where we went just once, before it closed its doors and lay empty for several years.

There were different truths about Eltham. The borough of Greenwich had an unenviable history of racist violence in the early and mid-1990s. Stephen himself had, aged just 15, worried his mother by insisting on going to Thamesmead, where racial tensions were running high, to take part in a protest at the racist murder of his contemporary Rolan Adams, also just 15, who Stephen had known a little. The purpose of the national BNP headquarters, up the road in Welling, was to ratchet up tensions, abetting the strutting of the now infamous Acourts and their racist gang. Many people wanted the reign of local terror exercised by the prime suspects to end. Any idea of a 'wall of silence' from the local community was a convenient myth to excuse the policing failure. The suspects' names had poured into the police inquiry from several directions the day after Stephen's murder. His brother Stuart has talked about deciding to carry on with school the next day – and coming home with the names too.

Eltham in 1999 mostly felt fairly safe to me, despite that ever-present shadow of its recent history. If it was after nine o'clock, I would take a very short cab ride from the station rather than walking home. I felt 99 per cent sure that was not always necessary, though 99 per cent is not always enough. It seemed worth the £4 fare anyway to avoid reopening that debate at home. Some pubs looked like a better choice than others if popping in to watch a half of Premiership football. I only had one direct experience of overt racism directed at me on the Well Hall Road. That was not at night, but not long before Saturday lunchtime, when I unfortunately caught the eye of a track-suited youth by the bus doors, already drinking his can of Fosters. 'Why don't you lot go back to where you came from?' he spat. I didn't think he meant Winchester. A decade earlier, in a school playground, I might have attempted a sarcastic riposte, but I just got past him, and off the bus, to return with my shopping to where I had come from. Home, which was, by then, after a short move up the road and around the corner, number 45 Shooters Hill.

Stacy was teaching dance and drama, holding lessons at the Frankie Howerd Hall and staging performances at the Bob Hope Theatre, venues whose names evoked a sense of local pride in those who had gone on to broader fame. The teenagers who choose to spend Saturdays and evenings singing and dancing were doubtless a different cohort to the knife-wielding Acourt gang, but she was always struck by their confidence and their lack of interest in racial difference; their easy friendships as an everyday fact. What Stacy's teenagers believed was more or less what Stephen Lawrence had believed too. Brian Cathcart's 1999 book *The Case of Stephen Lawrence* makes this core point well.[1] As an 18-year-old black Londoner in the early 1990s, Stephen Lawrence was used to navigating a world where almost everyone in power and authority was white, but did not see that as determining his prospects in life:

> Colour wasn't everything, he believed; black people like himself could usually do well and be happy if they were reasonably smart and avoided the obvious traps. And most of Britain, most of white Britain, was only too keen to agree with him and to believe that race and racism were diminishing concerns, and not nearly so bad, say, as in France and Germany. But Stephen was wrong. For him, on that day in southeast London, colour was everything.

Because Stephen was wrong about that, his grieving parents chose to bury him four thousand miles away in Jamaica. They believed that his grave would be safer there. That seemed a tragic indictment of our country. I did not want Stephen to belong primarily to Jamaica. He should have been, he was, one of us. But didn't that white paint on his memorial outside our front door – however quickly cleaned up, with new flowers, and however more vigilantly guarded second time around – show why they had a point?

What Stephen had expected was to be able to live his life: to catch his bus, to get home, to pursue a career and to make his contribution to Britain, as his parents had done, so that he might achieve more from the start that they had given him. What Stephen had believed was what I wanted and needed to believe. And so, if Stephen had been wrong about his expectation of being able to pursue his life in this country, his country, Britain, what mattered was that he should have been right. That may be the foundational reason why the campaign for justice for Stephen found such public resonance. Yet it is important, too, to consider why that took so long to happen.

How does change happen? The transformative power of unusual coalitions

It is 30 years since Stephen Lawrence was murdered. Next year will mark a quarter of a century since the 1999 Macpherson Report too. Stephen's story is now a landmark episode in the history of British relations. After the anti-racism protests of 2020, it seems natural today to think of Stephen Lawrence's case as Britain's own George Floyd moment, a generation earlier.

Each of those two very different murders would galvanise and shift the public conversation about race. In each case, what seemed a recurring, all too exhaustingly familiar story for some served as an eye-opening revelation for others. But it is worth reflecting on one crucial difference. The killing of Stephen Lawrence was a murder that would come to shock us all, eventually – but it was to take four years, rather than minutes or hours, for this murder to fully shake the conscience of our nation. There were no national newspaper or TV news headlines about this murder in the streets of south London in the days after it happened.

The campaign for justice for Stephen Lawrence forged unusual new alliances to tackle racism of a breadth never before seen in Britain. That had everything to do with the courage, commitment and tenacity of the Lawrences – unwilling to leave any stone unturned in challenging the failure of the police investigation – and the sheer breadth of the coalition that the parents mobilised.

That coalition included many race advocacy groups who had long campaigned against racism in the area, and lawyers who challenged the police's failures. The *Daily Mail* newspaper's swinging behind the campaign had a transformative impact. Its editor Paul Dacre responded viscerally to the swaggering sense of impunity of the prime suspects at the inquest, where each claimed privilege in refusing to answer any questions for fear of incriminating themselves. The inquest jury had taken just 30 minutes to unanimously decide that Stephen had been killed by 'a completely unprovoked racist attack by five white youths'. The *Mail's* front-page headline declared the five to be 'Murderers', laying down the gauntlet with 'The *Mail* accuses these men of killing. If we are wrong, let them sue us.'

People hold many different views of the *Daily Mail* newspaper. Because it was my mum's newspaper of choice, I formed several of my emerging views as a teenager as a foil to its strident claim to speak for Middle England. Yet that is what made the newspaper's making so much of the case so powerful. Its campaign was the most important example of aggressive tabloid journalism in pursuit of the public interest of my lifetime.

A change of government helped the Lawrences' campaign. New Home Secretary Jack Straw made the historic commitment to a public inquiry, having adopted the case in opposition, after meeting the Lawrences, and finding their case compelling. Recently published Cabinet papers show that Tony Blair's advisers in Downing Street were more sceptical of the proposed inquiry, worrying that this could raise expectations that could not be achieved and that 'even with good presentation look like an attack on the police'. That reflected New Labour's nervousness about race. There was very little ethnic diversity in the room where 'the project' was shaped. Because race was a topic intuitively associated with the party's left, the inner cities and the core vote, there was no similar electoral imperative as that which drove the New Labour push to shift the gender balance in parliament. Only 4 of Labour's newly elected 183 MPs of 1997 were from ethnic minorities, a similar proportion to those elected over the previous decade. Not that many people noticed, in 1997, that the New Labour Cabinet was all white, since every previous British Cabinet had been so too, though Paul Boateng was to become the first black British Cabinet minister, five years on, in 2002.

So, the *Daily Mail*'s stance helped create the political space to ensure that Jack Straw's proposal for a public inquiry should prevail. Its terms were narrowed, from a general review of police relations with black communities to lessons from racially motivated crime, though that theme was to broaden out again as the evidence was heard by the judge, his advisers and the public too.

Sir William Macpherson could be cast as an 'unusual ally'. The retired judge must have been a twenty-seventh generation Scot at least since, on his father's death in 1969, he had succeeded him to become the twenty-seventh Chief of the Clan Macpherson of Cluny, which stretched back more than 11 centuries to 843 and the time of Kenneth MacAlpin, first King of the Scots. The name of Sir William Macpherson was greeted with scepticism by the Lawrences and their supporters. Could this scion of the British Establishment, from the high gentry of the Scottish borders, understand how black British people felt about the way in which they were treated by the police? Jack Straw insisted that they had no veto of the appointment and would have to give Macpherson a chance. 'How wrong people were', wrote the barrister Hashi Mohamed, who conducted Macpherson's first interview about the report in many years, two decades later.[2] 'The nation was compelled to interrogate its soul and come to terms with uncomfortable truths about deeply embedded prejudices', he continued.[3]

Looking back at the history now, the role of chance and coincidence looms large. It had been a remarkable coincidence that the *Daily Mail* editor happened to know the Lawrences, since Stephen's father had done some decorating for him. The newspaper's first coverage of the case had been a somewhat sceptical account of Nelson Mandela's effort to raise its profile, under the headline 'How Race Militants Hijacked a Tragedy', in May 1993, a month after the murder. It was Neville Lawrence's challenge to that report that led to a more sympathetic account. As Doreen Lawrence wrote in her autobiography: 'The *Daily Mail's* front page had helped to open the story up ... that report was said to have "touched Middle England", the feelings of white people who don't normally care much what happens to black youths in inner cities.'[4] Many in Middle England, often for the first time, saw the issue of policing through the eyes of this black family, the murder of a teenager, the grief of his parents, and the injustice at this failure to bring justice.

Stephen Lawrence was one of two black teenagers waiting for that number 161 bus on the Well Hall Road on that fateful night. He was with his friend Duwayne Brooks. The Met acknowledged at the inquiry that they had never supported him properly. That was more than a sin of omission. Brooks' own book *Steve and Me* offers a jaw-dropping account of a gruelling campaign of harassment, while the stalled murder inquiry went nowhere, damaged by the additional pressure put on a vulnerable witness. (Brooks was later awarded damages from the Met.[5])

The most sobering thought, though almost certainly true, is that had Duwayne been murdered and his friend Stephen survived as a traumatised witness, the events that were to change social, political and legal history would have been much less likely to have happened. Duwayne Brooks would not have had the family back-story that the media and the public found compelling about Stephen's story. The case would have been just one more crime statistic. There have been many other cases – such as the murder of Surjit Singh Chhokar in Lanarkshire in 1998, for which nobody was convicted. It is uncomfortable to consider how capricious our attention to justice and injustice can be, and how much chance and contingency loom large. But it does make it all the more urgent to work out how those searing flashpoints that can briefly capture the national conscience so powerfully can be channelled in ways that might generate sustained change.

Where the 'institutional racism' conversation gets stuck

The Macpherson Report achieved more than Lord Scarman's inquiry into Brixton had a generation before. It delivered important advances, though other things were left undone. The report influenced the culture and practice of policing in many ways – from crime scene management to family liaison, though progress in diverse recruitment to the police remained slow, and led to new race equality duties in the public sector.[6] Yet a generation on, the Casey Review's finding of institutional racism, sexism and homophobia captured starkly just how much still needed to change.

The strength of the Macpherson Report was its focus on institutions, not just intentions. Its key argument was that unfair outcomes do not only result from malign intentions. This is why the idea of 'institutional racism' was central to its analysis. Macpherson's definition stands the test of time. 'The collective failure of an organisation to provide an appropriate and professional service to people because of their colour, culture or ethnic origin. It can be seen or detected in processes, attitudes and behaviour which amount to discrimination through unwitting prejudice, ignorance, thoughtlessness and racial stereotyping.'[7]

Looking back, I am struck by how often the way we talk about 'institutional racism' may hinder rather than help us to achieve our core purpose – to shift our attention towards institutions. What it needs us to do is to focus on the 'i word' – institutional – which is important, if rather boring. The 'i word' asks us to get serious by focusing on the serious, sustained work of institutional reform and change. Yet it simply lacks all of the emotional power and punch of the 'r word', racism, that it is paired with. The punch of the r-word gives talking about institutional racism some power and potency for media and political scrutiny, and for civic society campaigning too. But its impact arises mostly from its potency as a 'gotcha' question. A failure to own the label suggests evasion and denial, and yet adopting the label seems to me to have significant limits as a way to drive a sustained programme of change.

Like the defensive policemen in my kitchen back in 1999, most of us still mostly intuitively associate that red hot r-word with intentions, not institutions. That makes 'we are institutionally racist' sound intuitively to many listeners like it is saying 'we are rotten to the core'. That is a source of shame and guilt – intended as a route to drive change, though it may also distract from it. Institutions that want to commit to change will always struggle to apply the dreaded r-word to themselves and their efforts to address the disparities and exclusions that remain.

Though some may castigate any such defensiveness as a form of 'white fragility', we ought to hope to find institutional leaders of all colours and creeds grappling with these issues in this generation, such as the Prime Minister, or Lord Patel, the British Asian peer, who tried to grapple with the challenge of change at Yorkshire Cricket Club after its racism crisis during his brief tenure. There is an inherent tension for any institution, under any leadership, if we expect, for example, a university vice-chancellor to declare both that 'the University of Anytown aspires to be inclusive and fair to all' yet also to simultaneously declare that 'the University of Anytown is institutionally racist' as a core litmus test of taking the challenges of inclusion seriously. This appears to set up a binary state of grace or disgrace: 'Are we institutionally racist or not?' Yet the work of institutional reform is bound to remain an ongoing and constant work in progress, about the need to acknowledge the challenges, and the gaps, and to commit to the sustained work needed to narrow the gaps and move closer to the vision of fairness for all.

If what we are trying to get to is the i-word, then to secure a serious acknowledgement, along the lines that 'we recognise that disparities and discrimination require systemic change, and will take sustained work', it would help to try to use a less red-hot, cooler and more constructively useful term than the r-word, so that we can engage with the challenges of institutional discrimination and institutional disparities in a sustained way.

Old hatreds and new hatreds

On a summer's night in July 2005, in Huyton on Merseyside, another black British 18-year-old A-level student was looking for a bus home. Having been racially abused and threatened at the bus stop, Anthony Walker walked off to try another stop instead. Yet he was followed by a car and killed by a savage blow with an ice-pick to the head.

If Anthony Walker's brutal murder evoked that of Stephen Lawrence, a dozen years earlier, the police investigation was very different. The prime suspects were arrested within a week and convicted of murder within six months, receiving mandatory life sentences, for what the judge called 'a racist attack of a type poisonous to any civilised society'. Anthony's mother Gee Walker even said she could accept the remorse and guilty plea of the killer who had struck the fatal blow. 'I admire him for that … his mum must have instilled some goodness in him,' she said.

This was post-Macpherson progress of a kind, in that the police and courts did what they could, after the event, to mete out justice. But another black British young man of extraordinary promise had lost everything in a few blurred seconds to an unprovoked racist attack. A fairer justice and policing system is not enough without more progress against hatred. None of us can escape a one-in-a-million chance of being a murder victim. With 600 murders a year, the population-wide average would be ten in a million – but that is very unevenly distributed by gender and age, by social class and ethnic group. Black people are five times as likely to be murder victims.

The Macpherson Inquiry changed policing, substantially, though further challenges remain. Forty years after Scarman, a quarter of a century after Macpherson, progress towards police forces reflecting the communities they serve remains slow. On ethnic diversity, the only force to come close to matching the ethnic make-up of the public it serves is in Lincolnshire, the least diverse area, where 2 per cent of the police force and 2 per cent of the public are from visible minorities. There were stark and wide disparities in every region with average or above-average levels of ethnic diversity, particularly in the West Midlands and London.

Yet alongside this important, necessary focus on the institutional response of the police, the root cause of Stephen Lawrence's murder was racial hatred. Macpherson recognised this in the following powerful and acerbic passage, noting that while the police's failure meant that the case against the suspects was 'not proved', the racial hatred underpinning the crime certainly was.

They remain, however, prime suspects. And the nature of them in 1994, and indeed during their limited testimony in 1998, must surely make us all determined that by education, family and community influence, proper policing and all available means, society does all it can to ensure that the minds of present and future generations are not allowed to become violent and maliciously prejudiced. If these suspects were not involved there must have been five or six almost identical young thugs at large on the night of 22 April 1993 to commit this terrible racist crime. We must all see to it that such crimes do not and cannot happen again.[8]

There was eventually, and unexpectedly, a measure of justice for Stephen Lawrence, with the conviction of two of his murderers. The stalwart effort of Chief Inspector Clive Driscoll discovered new forensic evidence – a spot of Stephen's blood on the jacket of David Norris, providing an indelible trace of contact and proof of guilt. So the 2012 trial now replayed once again in the courtroom stories and scenes that had entered British culture –

from news reports to documentaries, the stage and television dramas. We saw the police flounder, and we saw how their unwitting assumptions contributed to that. 'Institutional racism' was an unfamiliar phrase then, but people knew what it was when they saw it.

Macpherson's reference to 'the nature of them' referred to the shocking surveillance footage collected by the police during their second investigation in 1994. That the suspects joke about being under surveillance (going out to use pay-phones for other conversations) makes what they were recorded saying all the more striking.

Luke Knight, from undercover CCTV footage, pays tribute to what he understood to be the gist of Enoch Powell's argument.

D'ya remember Enoch Powell? That geezer, he knew straight away, he went over to Africa and all that … he knew it was a slum, he knew it was a shithole and he came back here saying they're uncivilised and all that, and then they started coming over here and he knew, he knew straight away, he was saying, no, I don't want them here, no fucking niggers, they'll ruin the gaff and he was right, they fucking have ruined it.

David Norris and Neil Acourt fantasise in even more vitriolic terms about committing racist murders – even though they have already participated in one. 'If I was going to kill myself, do you know what I'd do? I'd go and kill every black cunt, every Paki, every copper … I'd go down Catford and places like that with two sub-machine guns,' says Norris.[9]

Those videos capture that the racial hatred was not just violent but territorial too. Britain has changed over the 30 years since Stephen Lawrence died. Eltham changed too, at first gradually and then more quickly. Over a third of the population is black, Asian or mixed race now, compared to around 6 per cent in

1993. This is a less racist society than the one in which Stephen Lawrence was killed. Yet we can still risk going backwards as well as forwards when it comes to race hatred. There has been a generational shift on hatred and prejudice, in south London, and more widely across the country.[10]

There are new dangers too. Poisonous narratives of the Great Replacement Theory combine with new opportunities online to socialise young men towards violence. New online dynamics create a paradox of racism. There are fewer racists in our society than there were 25 years ago, due to shifting social norms across generations. Yet I receive much more racist abuse in the 2020s than I did in the 1990s. Technology reduces the distance between us, so any ethnic minority figure with any public profile is one click away from some of the worst bigots. The frequency and intimacy of online racism corrodes faith, especially among young adults, in the real progress there has been on race and hatred since Stephen Lawrence's death.

The death of Stephen Lawrence changed Britain. In large part that was because Doreen Lawrence represents an important form of patriotism: the patriotism of dissent, the challenge to injustice, and the insistence on change. Hers was a challenge to injustice that opened many eyes. The justice of that challenge was recognised in the sense of public duty of Sir William Macpherson and others, who came to see that this was not simply an individual tragedy, caused by the almost incomprehensible hatred of his killers. It was also an injustice that changed the national conversation, creating a recognition of why institutions need to change to bring the ideals we would like to think our country must stand for closer to the lived experience of Britain today.

6

Faith

Divided loyalties or common ground

Being half-Irish was at least as important to me as being half-Indian when I was growing up. It was partly the attraction of an identity that you have to declare for yourself. But it was largely a question of faith.

I grew up as an Irish Catholic, albeit part of the small, if growing, mixed-race, Indian-Irish branch. My mother had stronger religious convictions than my dad, and Rome competed tenaciously for the children of mixed relationships. The Church would marry a Catholic and a non-Catholic, as long as the Catholic parent followed the catechism of promising to do all they could to bring up the children as Catholics. My dad chose to convert to Catholicism too. It was less clear whether he ever gave up his cultural identity as a Hindu, as he pioneered his own pantheistic mash-up of Ganesh and the Holy Trinity. So he took us to church every Sunday while also having some Hindu icons in the house. When his mother visited England, she would make small offerings of coconut on the beach, just under Southend Pier, as if it was the River Ganges itself rather than the Thames estuary. That was a sign of faith.

I saw the Pope come to Liverpool when I was seven. I was an altar boy, too. As the smallest in the group, I got to carry the baby Jesus to the crib for Midnight Mass on Christmas Eve. I did Irish dancing for a few years too, even participating in a large group number at the 1984 Liverpool International Garden Festival, an event that proved the most popular initiative of the various efforts to regenerate Merseyside. I was confirmed into the Catholic Church aged around 16 – taking the confirmation name Patrick – but talking it through in the confirmation group led to me falling out of the Church not long afterwards. Some emphasis was placed on resisting the temptation to be a 'cafeteria Catholic', a pejorative phrase for those proud enough to think they could pick and choose Catholic doctrines. For a teenager with a growing number of doubts about the patchy historic and contemporary track record of my infallible Church, it sounded like an invitation to exit. Maybe I would have kept going a bit longer if I had been a high-church Anglican.

My wife was also a lapsed Irish Catholic, so we had a civil wedding ceremony when we got married in Essex, with readings from poems by Yeats and Tagore. We did get our first child baptised as a Catholic, though this involved being asked by something of an Irish whiskey priest a couple of times if we would like to get ourselves 'properly married' while we were about it. At the baptism itself, I remember being again struck by how strongly the ceremony centred on the repudiation of Satan. We held civil naming ceremonies for our younger children.

Losing my religion seemed rather on trend. The Britain of the 1990s was secularising at pace. This was a story of generational change. Two religious parents had a 50–50 chance of passing their faith on, with one parent of faith having about half of that transmission rate. Only 6 per cent of those brought up without a religious faith acquire it. Half the population could be found in church in the nineteenth century, but that is closer to one in twenty people today. So Britain was increasingly coming to think of itself as a secular society with a Christian heritage and increasing multi-faith diversity around the edges.

That was the dynamic behind the long-term shift across generations that saw those who identified as Christian fall to 46 per cent of England and Wales in the 2021 census results, from six out of ten a decade earlier, while those answering that they had no religion rose to 37 per cent, with non-Christian faiths making up a tenth of the population. The symbolism of Christianity falling below 50 per cent grabbed the headlines. Every faith is a minority faith now, even nominally. Yet while the settled population was secularising at speed, generations of immigration were slowing down the secularisation of Britain or bringing faith back into British society. Italian, Irish and Polish migrants kept the Catholic Church going. Black Christians are about three times as likely to attend church as white people who identify as Christian. Fifty years ago, Jews – around 1 out of 150 people in Britain – comprised the largest non-Christian minority faith in Britain. With four million Muslims, a million Hindus, 500,000 Sikhs and over 250,000 Jews, Britain had become a country of many faiths and none.

The census headlines sometimes suggested a Brexit-style tug-of-war over whether Britain should be defined as a post-Christian and post-religious society – as Christian identification fell below half, with faith identity remaining in a slim majority. When twenty-seven million people continue to identify as Christian – around a quarter of whom are regular Church-goers – while six million identify with non-Christian faiths, and twenty-two million state that they have no religion, the question is more how to now achieve the right boundaries and relationships to live together well in this mixed and plural society.

Over time, Britain had evolved an unusual semi-secularism, with an Established Church, albeit one often caricatured as bordering on the agnostic and with bishops sitting by right in the legislature, but faith seemed to be gently settling more into the dignified rather than the efficient part of the Constitution. Strong support for the freedom of religion in principle was honoured in practice more in the breach than the observance. Democracies that attempted a much stricter separation of Church and State, like the American and French Republics, often had more religiosity in public life and sharper clashes about how to police the boundary of the scope and limits of faith in society. Those clashes were coming back to Britain too. Arguments about this became central to many of the public controversies of this century. The 'New Atheism' of Richard Dawkins and allies challenged *The God Delusion*, as the title of Dawkins' book put it, seeing the public recognition of faith as an affront to reason, though this aggressive variant of secularism drifted into online trolling. The compatibility, or otherwise, of Islam with Western societies became the central integration issue across Western democracies. Anti-Semitism became a more central political theme than it had been for 30 years, with the Labour Party being formally censured by the Equalities and Human Rights Commission over its failure to uphold its legal duties to tackle it. What it now meant to be British would depend on whether we could work out how to have a common citizenship, a shared identity, and to live well together in a society of many faiths and none.

Old and new suspicions

Very little of this was about Catholicism any more. Being an Irish Catholic in Britain got much easier in the 1990s. For my Irish mother-in-law, the hunger strikes of 1981 – when Bobby Sands was elected as a member of parliament on an 86 per cent turnout in Fermanagh, halfway through two months of starving himself to death, felt like the most heightened moment. A decade later, the release of the Guildford Four felt like a useful turning point, belatedly recognising the dangers and injustices that could arise from the sweeping suspicion that Catholics with an Irish accent must have more than a grudging regard for the IRA. After the Good Friday Agreement, much of the heat came off the Irish and the Catholics, and fell instead much more on Britain's Muslims.

I could certainly hear clear echoes of that long but now fading history of anti-Catholic discrimination in the English suspicion of Islam. The broader question was again whether supranational loyalty to a higher power, whether the Vatican or the Ummah, meant divided loyalties. Having experienced an increase in the status and standing of mixed-race Britons too, I felt some empathy for the minority group for whom things seemed to be going in the opposite direction – increasingly placed under a 'them and us' spotlight about whether this suspicious out-group could ever be truly us.

Islam has had a long presence in Britain. England's first purpose-built mosque, Woking's magnificent Shah Jahan Mosque, was constructed in Surrey in 1889. It was a century later that the Rushdie affair, revolving around the publication of his book, *The Satanic Verses*, catapulted the Muslim presence and the question of Islam in Britain to the centre of public controversy as never before. The book was burnt in Bradford in January 1989 shortly before the Ayatollah of Iran's Valentine's Day fatwa called for the death of the author.

Calls to ban the book produced a very binary debate. Necessarily so. There was next to no scope for middle ground between the author's claim for free expression – 'if you don't want to read a book, you don't have to read it' – and arguments, theological or political, that the depth of offence to a faith or its adherents should trump that. I thought then, as I think now, that the staunch defence of the right to publish, and so to defend the right to offend, was essential.

There was much vocal support for the author, though the theme of an ungrateful migrant bringing other people's conflicts to Britain was a recurring undertone. Norman Tebbit could never quite see the author as British: 'How many societies having been so treated by a foreigner accepted in their midst, could go so far to protect him from the consequences of his egotistical and self-opinionated attack on the religion into which he was born?' he asked.[1]

Historian Hugh Trevor-Roper could even gleefully fantasise about violence against the author in the pages of *The Independent*.[2] Having eventually got some of his life back, after the Iranian government downgraded the fatwa in 1998, Rushdie, in 2022, was to suffer a life-threatening attack in New York, by a 24-year-old, born years after the fatwa itself. I was disappointed much earlier that Shirley Williams, from the liberal centre, did not defend Rushdie's knighthood on *Question Time* in 2007, almost two decades after the fatwa, leaving Christopher Hitchens to explain why so many Muslim writers and intellectuals took the author's side against theocratic authoritarianism. If any British writer deserved a knighthood, Rushdie did. *Midnight's Children* had not just won the Booker of Bookers. It had also sparked a new branch of English and Commonwealth literature in India. Yet by the time Rushdie was elevated to Companion of Honour in the Jubilee honours of 2022, there were no public objections in Britain.

The Rushdie affair exposed the depth of disconnection between Britain's institutions and a million and a half Muslims in Britain. There were no Muslims at all in the House of Commons, and barely any in our newsrooms. There were no national Muslim civic groups. It was unfortunate that Britain's sole Asian MP was Keith Vaz, a British Indian Christian of Goan heritage, elected in Leicester less than two years beforehand. Salman Rushdie later recalled in his memoir how Vaz offered him his full support in a telephone call, a fortnight before leading a march of Muslims in Leicester calling for the book to be banned. Vaz later argued that what he was attempting to do was to channel Muslim anger into the political process. 'As with any political campaign, tactics are changed and learnt. Thus a petition to Parliament about the blasphemy laws is circulating in the mosques', he wrote in *The Guardian* a year on from the fatwa.[3] It was an awkward fact for Salman Rushdie's staunch liberal allies that UK common law did prohibit blasphemy, and, though widely considered archaic, had been successfully used in one private prosecution in 1977. (The law was finally repealed in 2008.)

I never did read *The Satanic Verses*. Because I was heading to India the next summer, for the first time as a teenager, I was soon to embark on *Midnight's Children*, Rushdie's epic magic realist reimagination of the making of modern India. That was the Rushdie book that came to matter most to me. But I did follow many of the author's other attempts to escape the strait-jacket of having become a *cause célèbre* and to return to being an author who wanted to explore his themes of crossed borders, complexity and the ambiguities of in-betweenness. Perhaps it was in that spirit that I saw no contradiction in being on the side of Salman Rushdie, and on the side of British Muslims too, if one could find the right allies, which is what I tried to do in the years after 9/11 and 7/7.

The Muslim bridgers

The strength of the 'them and us' debate about Islam in Britain made the decade after 2005 a difficult time to be a British Muslim bridger: one of those who believed that Britain and Islam were compatible, and who wanted to see off Islamist extremism and anti-Muslim prejudice. It meant that there was a difficult but necessary conversation to tackle the scepticism across British society about the integration and even the shared allegiance of our Muslim fellow citizens and Muslim anxiety about the barriers to equal opportunity, status and respect in British society, where Muslims face extra hurdles and suspicions.

When terrorists attacked trains and buses taking Londoners to work, the victims were from every faith, ethnicity and social class. That the bombers were home-grown was what most shook the confidence of British society. How could young people who were born, grew up and went to school here in the UK prefer what is on offer from al-Qaeda and its offshoots to the sense of belonging on offer in British society?

This battle for British Islam had to involve more than a 'counter-narrative'. Most mainstream Western politicians made the essential distinctions between the extremist forms of political Islamism that underpinned and sought to inspire terrorist violence and the faith of Islam itself. Yet pigeonholing our allies in media discourse as the 'moderate Muslims' risked conceding the authenticity of the faith to the extremists. If extremism makes a call to action, then the call to inaction of counter-extremism would not be enough. With three million Muslim fellow citizens, and half of them aged under 24, it was a problem if 'how do we stop you being an extremist?' seemed to be the first question that the state and their fellow citizens appeared to be asking about them. The ultimate answer had to be a home-grown British Islam, fully confident of its place and status in Britain, making its contribution to the common ground of equal and shared citizenship across all groups and individuals in our society.

As Professor Tariq Modood put it: 'The reaffirming of a plural, changing, inclusive British identity that can be as emotionally and politically meaningful to British Muslims as the appeal of *jihadi* sentiments is critical to isolating and defeating extremism.' If this was the mission, it had important implications for citizenship and identity for everybody else too. 'We cannot both ask new Britons to integrate and go around saying that being British is, thank goodness, a hollowed-out meaningless project whose time has come to an end', he added.[4]

For all of the pressure that British Muslims and the Muslim bridgers were under, these were two decades of integration. Where Muslims had been entirely absent from public life, there was a growing voice, visibility and presence. Sadiq Khan had been elected in Tooting in May 2005. 'I did not come into Parliament to be a Muslim MP', he was to write of his election as the Labour representative for Tooting, where he grew up. But when 7/7 happened just two months later, Khan was the only one of London's 73 MPs who was Muslim (and one of just four across the United Kingdom) he could hardly avoid the responsibility of playing his part. I worked closely with him at the Fabian Society that year, and across that parliament, along with former minister John Denham, who had resigned from government over the Iraq War, developing a 'fairness not favours' account of how to integrate issues of Muslim opportunity and integration into a broader framework of shared citizenship, equal opportunity and democratic voice.[5] A decade later, Khan was the elected Mayor of London and there were 19 British Muslim members of parliament by 2019. Most, ten, of them were women, though no British Muslim or Asian women had ever sat in the House of

Commons before May 2010. That progress came with challenges too. Nus Ghani, the first British Muslim female minister, alleged that discriminatory language was used when she was sacked, as Transport Minister, having been told that it had been her responsibility to vocally dismiss any issues of anti-Muslim prejudice within her party.

'British Islam is a noticeably broad church, and broadening still,' as Dr Timothy Winter of the University of Cambridge put it. He was speaking at the Woking mosque, whose gardens had been converted into a memorial burial ground, to honour the Muslims who had fought for Britain in two world wars, on the theme of 'Finding an English Islam'.[6] 'A local British Islam, or a range of British Islams, is religiously authentic and even mandatory ... Apart from those fundamentalist enclaves inspired by Saudi zealotry, younger British Muslims are very recognisably from and of their own place', he suggested. 'They carry the regional accents, they fully hear their colleagues and neighbours, and are understood in turn, and have clearly made themselves at home in some idiom of Britishness or even Englishness, whether in our hospitals, politics, media, or even academe.' Baroness Sayeeda Warsi, speaking at the same event, saw the importance of the regional: 'I've always described Islam as like a river, which takes its colour from the bed over which it flows – and my Islam flows over Yorkshire and over England,' she said. 'The river bed must know what it represents' too. 'For minority faiths to feel truly comfortable about who they are, the majority has got to be sure about who it is,' she concluded.

A 2022 survey of British Muslims from Savanta ComRes, published to launch the new online magazine *Hyphen*, captured a striking if little heard sense of growing confidence across Muslim Britain.[7] A majority of British Muslims said their lives were better than five years ago, that the next generation would do better than their parents, and that life as a Muslim in the UK was generally better than in other European societies. Seven out of ten respondents felt there were Muslim role models in British society, a development reflecting progress in business, culture, politics and sport. It is striking how unusual and overdue it seemed in 2015 to see someone like Nadiya Hussain – the daughter of a waiter from Bangladesh, a mother and talented cook – earning national treasure status as the winner of *The Great British Bake Off*. Yet for seven out of ten respondents, a broad confidence in increasingly equal opportunities was countered by having personally experienced prejudice or discrimination on account of their faith.

Anti-Muslim prejudice retains a much broader reach than most other forms of racism (alongside prejudice against those from a Traveller background). It can be the form of casual prejudice that still passes the 'dinner table test', as Sayeeda Warsi has put it. Claims and counter-claims about Islamophobia provide the sharpest arguments about the boundaries limiting free speech. 'Islamophobia' is now used by many people and institutions as a synonym for 'anti-Muslim prejudice', without seeing much or any differentiation between these ideas. This was an unfortunate shift in terminology. Having a label that centres the faith (Islam) rather than the people (Muslims) risks blurring this crucial boundary. Doing the work of challenging prejudice effectively may be more important than the label, but it makes it harder to build the broad coalition that is needed.

The essential distinction is that the critique of ideas – theological or political – is always to be defended, but that prejudice against followers of a religion is illegitimate. It is not Islamophobic to critique ideas and engage in robust political or theological debates, whether about Islam or any faith. But it crosses into prejudice if it criticises Muslims for being Muslim, stereotypes all Muslims, or is a debate on Muslims that Muslims themselves aren't expected to be part of.

The UK government committed to a process to build a consensus definition in 2019, under the late James Brokenshire, but did nothing to pursue this after the change of administration from Theresa May to Boris Johnson, leaving a foundational gap in efforts to tackle prejudice.

Another somewhat ironic and under-observed contributor to the quiet rise of Muslim confidence was, ironically, the breathing space offered by an outbreak of other big identity and culture debates. Identity debates in the decade after 7/7 were invariably a 'them and us' debate about Muslims. Those issues have not gone away, but it may be that the arguments about Brexit and Covid, Black Lives Matter and statues, sexuality, gender and trans rights meant that British Muslims were less exclusively on the frontline of the identity arguments in British society, in contrast to the French presidential election between the current president, Emmanuel Macron, and the candidate Marine Le Pen, in which Muslim integration often dominated the French public agenda.

Multiculturalism and its discontents

The Rushdie affair was one of a number of episodes that brought Britain's model of multiculturalism into question. Multiculturalism meant many different things to different people. Faith and ethnicity, nationality and language, were often used interchangeably to describe diverse 'cultures'. The public debate about 'multiculturalism' had become prominent in the 1960s when the primary question was still the Powellite one about whether to accept or reject the presence of ethnic diversity itself. One legacy of that period was how, even two generations later, supporters and mainstream critics of multiculturalism would often talk past each other, with very different ideas of what this meant.

For its advocates and defenders, talk about multiculturalism was still often primarily about recognising and embracing the *social fact* that Britain was now a multi-ethnic and multi-faith society. Most ethnic minority citizens tended to see it as a positive term, many feeling they had a stake in not just the idea but the reality of integration. Yet multicultural*ism* – properly understood – was not just about the social fact of a diverse Britain, but how policymakers should respond to that social fact of diversity.

There were many different multiculturalist projects. In his famous 1966 speech, Roy Jenkins had defined multiculturalism as 'not a flattening process of assimilation but as equal opportunity accompanied by cultural diversity, in an atmosphere of mutual tolerance'.[8] This was a case for multiculturalism as a means towards integration in a liberal society, with some emphasis of integration being a two-way street. But more cosmopolitan models of multiculturalism were more sceptical about the value of national identity or viewed integration as suspiciously assimilationist.

Multiculturalism in its various forms had a mixed record. It could claim a major positive achievement in the strength of British identity among British ethnic minorities. There were, though, three big reasons why the traditional model of multiculturalism would come under increasing pressure, and need to be rethought, by the end of the century, by emerging generations.

The first generation of British multiculturalism was developed in an era in which Britain's visible minorities were simply absent from the institutions of political, civic and cultural power. Jews and Catholics had managed to cross this insider/outsider boundary, but it took almost four decades after Windrush for there to be any black or Asian MPs in Westminster. Other institutions often lagged even further behind. Addressing these barriers to equal opportunity was of course a focus of advocacy for race equality. This absence from institutions was one major reason why British multiculturalism in practice often developed largely as a matter of 'multi-faithism' – the public recognition of minority faith communities. Yet the first two generations of practice of multicultural 'multi-faithism' proved an excessively male affair, nationally and locally. Too often, a naive 'take me to your leader' model of community relations paid too little attention to the share of voice, across genders, and also across generations, within minority groups.

It became increasingly important, also, to differentiate between ethnicity, faith and culture. The conflation of culture, faith and ethnicity could lead to apparent failures to apply the law without fear or favour, such as was the case with the Rochdale and Rotherham grooming scandals, either through misplaced concerns about 'cultural sensitivity' or a misogynistic council culture of disbelieving and not valuing the voice of young girls who were victims of sexual abuse.

I think the anxiety about discussing 'cultural factors' reflects the confusion that this must mean something like 'properties of an ethnic or faith group' and so risk generalising about or stereotyping whole groups at that level. (Ironically, this is in itself a racial group stereotype, by turning the behaviour of a criminal sub-group into a community characteristic.) It was a British Asian prosecutor, Nazir Afzal, who led the prosecutions of nine men involved in a grooming gang in Rochdale.

Consider the many other ways that we talk about cultural factors – the misogyny of trading floors, or in student rugby clubs, or Oxbridge dining societies. If, for example, the Bullingdon Club creates a sense of entitlement about smashing things up, that is a cultural norm among the sub-group of members, but not necessarily one shared by all privately educated Oxford students. Few people would find it difficult to question the role of cultural factors in the role of the Church in twentieth-century Ireland – and how that institutional culture affected responses to child protection, or abuse in the Church. If a culture of disbelief at Rotherham Council towards young girls who were victims of abuse is worth investigating, then the regressive attitudes among some South Asian men towards women needs to be challenged too.

A traditional 'community of communities' multiculturalism could suggest a federated model of faith and ethnic groups. It was perhaps more intuitively obvious to the mixed-race Indian-Irish lapsed Catholic agnostic that this might offer too neat, tidy and narrow a set of boxes for the third and fourth post-war generation. That would become a wider challenge by this decade, where those of mixed ethnic origins outnumber any particular minority group. A related but perhaps more difficult challenge was how the 'community of communities' model portrayed the white majority group, a challenge exacerbated by the rapid decline of Christian faith practice. The initial implicit assumption of the 1960s and 1970s was that a focus on minority contact and integration was important, because the majority was settled in its own identity. That intuition underestimated how, if identity mattered to minorities, it would matter to majorities too. Did a 'community of communities' model want the white majority to think of itself as having its own identity and group interests – or, if it did not, might that be the unintended consequence of an asymmetric multiculturalism?

In principle, the multiculturalist aim could be to develop a new, inclusive and civic national identity that is not ethnically defined. Yet it would be difficult to achieve that if the majority feel this 'multiculturalism' question is a debate for minorities, about minorities, and not about all of us together. If cultural recognition matters to both minorities and majorities, then the central focus should be on the confident, civic national identity we can all share.

So there were distinct critiques and challenges to multiculturalism 'from within'; from liberal, feminist and left voices who
sought to champion diversity and challenge discrimination, as
well as from more traditionally hostile and rejectionist forces. I
had published one of the first, Yasmin Alibhai-Brown's 'After
Multiculturalism', in a Foreign Policy Centre pamphlet in 2000,
which focused on the risk of multiculturalism freezing social
change beyond the first generation.[9] After the 2001 summer riots
in northern towns, Ted Cantle's concept of 'parallel lives' – two
communities living side by side, with little interaction or sympathy – reflected a common thread of the reports into the disorder
in Oldham, and later disturbances in Burnley, Bradford and
Leeds. The dominant critique of multiculturalist policy increasingly became that the emphasis on recognising difference could
end up incentivising it. This fed, too, a symbiotic relationship of
extremisms. The BNP shifted its focus. It was little surprise that
Anjem Choudary's various fronts and Tommy Robinson's English
Defence League grew up together in the playgrounds of Luton.
The Islamist extremists and the white far-right extremists needed
and fed off each other, helping each side to verify its 'them and
us' narrative of grievances to its target audience.

The leading multiculturalist academic Bhikhu Parekh's
conception in leading the influential but sharply contested
Commission on Multi-ethnic Britain at the turn of the century
was that Britain was 'a community of communities and a
community of citizens, both a liberal and a multicultural society,
and needs to reconcile their sometimes conflicting require-
ments'.[10] The Rushdie affair was one of a number of issues to test
this fault line within multiculturalism, as to how it would seek to
resolve clashes between liberal and communitarian claims. For
me, the Parekh formula ultimately offered too little guidance on
how clashes between the claims of individuals and groups would
be resolved.

The foundational principles should be liberal ones, while valuing all of the communitarian commitments that are compatible with and freely chosen within that framework, whether by individuals or by groups of citizens. That 'post-multiculturalist' rebalancing could unlock some of the latent common ground on substance across those different intuitions among ethnic minorities and majorities, and across left and right, as to whether multiculturalism itself is a 'hurrah!' (inclusion) or 'boo!' (segregation) word. Given the settled social fact of a multi-ethnic and multi-faith society, we should recognise and respect our differences, but work particularly to promote the things that could bring us together.

The future of multi-faith Britain

I would argue that we might best see modern Britain as a community of citizens, aspiring to realise a shared ideal of fair chances and equal status for citizens of every colour and creed, which requires us to respect, protect and champion both individual freedom of belief and the freedom of group association in our diverse and liberal society, while promoting a shared sense of identity, and an ethos of connection, care and mutual respect so that we can all live well together in our shared home. That is how we can both recognise and respect our diversity, and promote what we want to share in common.

Our new monarch King Charles III is a moderate multiculturalist. He has long spoken of how he sees Britain as a 'community of communities'. Among his first public statements as head of state was to declare his sense of a duty to protect diversity. 'It is the duty to protect the diversity of our country, including by protecting the space for faith itself and its practice through the religions, cultures, traditions and beliefs to which our hearts and minds direct us as individuals', recognising too the value of humanist and secular contributions.[11] This new duty, described by the King as 'less formally recognised but to be no less solemnly discharged', was a more evolutionary, gradualist change than Charles was entertaining in the mid-1990s when envisaging becoming 'defender of faith'. His oath and role as the Head of the Church of England remain, enabling the King to balance continuing commitment to Britain's Christian heritage with its multi-faith present. By emphasising that a collective commitment to 'freedom of conscience, generosity of spirit and care for others' are essential to make diversity work and are 'the essence of our nationhood', this is a statement that recognises the importance of shared commitments too.

This public recognition of faith – both our Christian heritage, and our multi-faith present – can be valuable, as long as humanist and secular perspectives are recognised as legitimate forms to think about the ethics of the good life and the good society.

The role of government is to get the foundations and boundaries right. The foundational British value of the freedom of belief must protect the rights of both believers and non-believers, including the right to exit. Faith groups are communities of belief with a shared purpose that seek to transmit values and rituals across generations. There is a public interest in influencing which versions within different faith traditions emerge, evolve and prosper, welcoming the constructive contribution of those strands of thought committed to the common good and to good relations across communities.

One key change would be to systematically ensure a balance of voices by gender, by generation and by other relevant demographics in all forms of public engagement by national and local government, public services and others. As the Women's Faith Forum has set out, when faith groups are being consulted formally or informally, those responsible for the consultation have a duty to ensure that women are equally represented, which means more than simply being half the people in the 'room'. This principle should be applied by generation as well as by gender. It should not prevent older, male voices being heard too, as long as that is much closer to a quarter of the share of voice across genders and generations, overcoming any residual legacy of historic claims to speak for whole communities or of the type of gatekeeping that seeks to veto the participation of others.

As the new King was making his remarks to faith leaders about his vision for a 'community of communities', there were tensions on the streets of Leicester between groups of young men drawn from the city's Asian Hindu and Muslim communities. By the time the Leicester tensions gained national attention, two 'parallel narratives', of two diametrically opposed stories of villains and victims had arisen: of the importation of Hindu Nationalist politics to intimidate local Muslims, or alternatively of there being a 'Hinduphobic' effort by Muslims to make Hindus scared to practise their faith in Britain. Many civic voices within Leicester behaved responsibly, with women in particular seeking to ensure their voices were heard. But actors outside the city were primarily invested in choosing one of the parallel narratives to project so as to confirm and reinforce the pre-existing views, suspicions and biases of their different target audiences at home and abroad. These parallel narratives were spreading nationally too. Their share of voice no doubt differed in areas with a significant Muslim or Hindu presence, but little organic contact with the other group, from mixed areas where both groups were present in significant numbers.

Leicester had long thought of itself as a model of how to make diversity work in British cities. It has often been referred to as Britain's first 'majority-minority' city, but it turned out rather to be a city in which there was no majority group. The white British group made up the largest single group, while a variety of British

Indian communities were, overall, of a similar size, alongside smaller groups of British Pakistani origin. In faith terms, around a third of the population were Christian, one in five Muslim and one in six Hindu, with about one in twenty-five being Sikh. When Idi Amin was expelling the Ugandan Asians in 1972, the city council took out advertisements imploring people not to come to Leicester. Half a century later, Leicester was the centre of efforts to celebrate the Ugandan Asian contribution to Britain.

That half-century was not without its challenges and tensions, though the targeting of the city and county by the National Front in the 1970s and the BNP in the 1990s proved to be a source of solidarity across communities. 'Those common experiences forged strong relationships between first generation migrants to Leicester – including confronting racism that could not and did not discern between Hindu, Muslim and Sikh', Dilwar Hussain, founder of New Horizons in British Islam, and a Leicester resident for a quarter of a century, told me. But newer arrivals were not necessarily part of that shared patchwork, while younger generations growing up in an era of shifting international politics and more polarised identity clashes online may have less time for the 'keep calm and carry on' message of their elders. This meant that more efforts to create stronger relationships in schools, going beyond places of worship, were needed.

I am sure that faith schools are here to stay for the foreseeable future. It is difficult to imagine any democratic government would be able to dissolve them, as a matter of social and electoral reality. The privilege or running such schools now extends across all major faiths – Church of England, Catholic and Jewish schools joined by Muslim, Hindu and Sikh ones – and it comes with a clear and practical responsibility to educate children for a shared society. The practical way to do this is to expect every school in Britain, whether a faith school or not, to promote good community relations, with a responsibility for governing bodies to consider their strategies for fulfilling this regularly. I would favour a more voluntarist than prescriptive model for how to do that. While the everyday lived reality of many classrooms and playgrounds may make this straightforward in many areas, a broader regional and national effort could help schools make connections: for example, in the least diverse areas, or where demographic patterns make connections between different minority groups (such as between Muslims and Jews or Hindus) less likely to arise organically.

Faith institutions can play an influential role as convenors and practitioners, and can be champions of positive relations. Yet ensuring good relations in a diverse society would not place quite such an excessive expectation on faith leaders in minority communities to be the primary navigators of the rapid shifts between the generations in minority communities, or of the ties that bind a liberal and diverse society together.

7

Brexit in Billericay

**Why did Brexit divide us so deeply
(and can we get beyond it now?)**

'I don't feel like compromising. This is the first time I've won for forty years.' It is 2019 and my father-in-law, Sam, is not happy. He has been sent a polling card for the local elections. 'Do you know what I am thinking of doing, Sunder?' he asks me. 'I feel like sending this back with a note saying "Please don't send me any more of these things until you have done the last thing that we voted for."'

We are in Billericay in Essex, where my in-laws Sam and Kathy live. About seven out of ten people voted to leave the European Union around here, including them. Sam agrees that the electoral registrar at Chelmsford County Hall is probably the wrong scapegoat for his frustration about the stalemate over Brexit in parliament. His threat to leave the electorate is short-lived, because there is another polling card too. Sam thinks the right response to the invitation to vote in a European Parliament election – three years after the British referendum, which voted to leave – would be to become a conscientious objector in future elections. But he will definitely cast a vote in that one, for Nigel

Farage's Brexit Party, to send a simple message to Westminster that the politicians need to get on and do what the public voted for.

Brexit divided Britain deeply. People disagreed on the choice put to them on the ballot paper: whether to leave or remain in the European Union. It illuminated deeper rifts over the social and economic changes of recent decades. Yet its aftermath exacerbated them too, especially because Brexit created two new 'them and us' identities, the Remainers and Leavers, which became among the most important political and even social identities that many people had. The two tribes offered parallel, incompatible accounts of what was going on, and who was to blame for what seemed to be becoming an ever-deepening divide.

I understood a lot more about the depth of those divides from talking to the in-laws in Billericay about it, especially during that long stalemate from 2016 to 2019. I had cast my own referendum vote on the other side of the argument from them. But that did not mean we disagreed on everything. I did think that Sam and Kathy were right on one foundational point. The morning after that 52 to 48 per cent result was in, I could see that it was important that Britain should leave the European Union. The next debate would be about what form Brexit should take. What I didn't agree with was the conviction in Billericay that Britain could simply leave without any kind of deal at all. Leaving with a deal did not feel to Sam like the sort of compromise that he wanted to make; negotiating with the EU over exit terms felt as though we still needed permission to depart. This view was softened by the belief that there would be a much greater willingness to then agree all of the sensible practical arrangements that would need to follow a no-deal exit, if we could just get past the political stand-off with a clean break, so that trade and life could go on without unnecessary disruption. That sounded quite like a deal to me.

The in-laws even ditched their newspaper of 30 years – the *Daily Mail* – because of how strongly it was promoting Theresa May's Brexit deal. Kathy felt let down by Theresa May. 'It embarrasses me that she is a woman. I thought that once they put a female Prime Minister in, she would get the job done. She has been there two or three years – and they have got nothing to show for it,' she said. She did not think that you could get away with that in any other job. Boycotting the *Daily Mail* for being insufficiently Eurosceptic may seem to show an unusual strength of feeling on the issue. To be fair, the specific trigger was the newspaper's direct attacks on those who opposed the deal, characterising them as wreckers and saboteurs, which both Kathy and Sam found insulting. 'The editor has changed – the new editor is an idiot,' Sam told me, having noticed the shift in the newspaper's editorial voice after Paul Dacre was replaced by Geordie Greig. So *The Times* replaced the *Daily Mail* in Billericay for a few months. Sam told me that, while the paper of record was a good deal more expensive, it was much better value. 'I read almost the whole thing, cover to cover. The obituaries are especially good.' Kathy seemed less convinced by that change. The *Daily Mail* came back into favour in Billericay after the change of Prime Minister in 2019.

The in-laws voted for Boris Johnson in that General Election. They disapproved of Nigel Farage's decision to withdraw his Brexit Party candidates, because that felt a bit patronising. They could have made the decision not to vote for the Brexit Party in a General Election for themselves. This also took away any semblance of drama from the election campaign in Essex, making it simply a question of waiting to hear what the rest of the country would decide. The in-laws found themselves on the winning side, but this was far from unusual. Whatever the strength of views on Brexit, they turned out to be bell-weather swing voters in General Elections. They had switched their vote to Margaret

Thatcher, but were deeply disillusioned with John Major during the 1992 recession, switching to New Labour and the Liberal Democrats in the Blair era, but preferring David Cameron to Gordon Brown. During the 1997 election, they had been members of the Conservative Club in Castle Point, where harassed local MP Bob Spink complained that those in the club should be out knocking on doors. Sam's response – 'Campaign for you? I don't think anybody here is voting for you' – saw the stressed MP chucking out most members of the club a few nights before polling day. That was an omen that he was about to lose his 16,000 majority, as New Labour won the seat from third place in one of its unlikeliest gains of that landslide election.

I came to understand that the in-laws had a rather effective, somewhat plebiscitary theory of political change: the key question was whether to re-elect the incumbent or to chuck them out, using whatever alternative was to hand. For all that Sam felt like he had never won before, having been on the losing side in the 1975 referendum, it had been unusual for anybody to arrive in Downing Street without their votes in the decades since.

An (unfashionable) defence of the EU referendum

Many people who regret Brexit have a simple explanation: blame David Cameron. The former Prime Minister is charged with sacrificing a vital national interest for internal party management, because he failed to recognise the dangerous simplicities of direct democracy.

David Cameron gambled politically and lost. He overestimated his own persuasive powers and ended his premiership. But I do not find the idea that all of this trouble could have been avoided, simply by not holding a referendum, at all persuasive. Simply as a counter-factual scenario, it seems difficult to sustain the idea that a referendum could have been long avoided after 2014, certainly under almost any conceivable Conservative-led government. There may be much to criticise in how the referendum was won and lost, and especially in how both the winners and losers responded to the close result. But I think the somewhat unfashionable case that the referendum was necessary, and probably unavoidable, remains fairly strong.

A blanket case against referendums is too simplistic. They are the only legitimate way to settle some kinds of political question, especially those with the highest stakes. As the United Kingdom is now explicitly a Union of consent, questions about which state to be part of will require referendums to ratify any future change. The Good Friday settlement recognises that potential route to Irish reunification. The 1998 referendums on the Good Friday Agreement, in both Northern Ireland and the Republic, offer a paradigm example of the constructive use of referendums to entrench a fragile political agreement in broad public consent. Other referendums – on Scottish and Welsh devolution, a Mayor for London, and the largely forgotten 2011 referendum on electoral reform – demonstrate an emerging practice of setting big 'rules of the game' issues about the constitutional framework by referendums, without using them for domestic policy issues, like tax, climate change or the NHS.

One risk of the 2016 referendum was to amplify tensions between direct and representative democracy. Yet the decision to hold an EU referendum was clearly a product of our representative democracy. It arose from pressure in parliament and contested arguments within and between parties. The Commons finally voted by 544 votes to 53 to hold the referendum (though most of those voting for it would be advocating a Remain vote) because opposition MPs recognised that parties advocating a referendum had won a majority of both seats and votes in the 2015 General Election. On the eve of the referendum, 66 per cent of the public, including most Remain voters, thought it was the right way to settle the question while 24 per cent thought it was a bad choice. (There was a still-narrower majority – by 55 per cent to 33 per cent – days later once the result was known.[1]) The wide margin of that Commons vote makes it impossible to deny that, as a political community, those on different sides of the Brexit argument did agree that a referendum would settle this question. As David Cameron recognised in his resignation speech, the morning after the leave vote was confirmed, those who supported holding the vote had a responsibility to enact the result, however disappointed they might be. David Cameron's error was less in holding the referendum, more in losing it.

How the referendum was won and lost

Either side could have won or lost the EU referendum. Two-quarters of the public – one-quarter on each side of the question – never had any doubts how they would vote if this question was put to them. Sam in Billericay saw no need to rethink the decision he had made in 1975: 'if the rest of you had listened to me then, we could have saved forty years of trouble'. There was equal conviction, on the other side, that staying in the EU was the only sensible choice. But if each side had up to 30 per cent of the electorate locked down from the start, each faced a real struggle to persuade a majority.

Remain won the argument about the economic pros and cons with most graduates, who voted by about 3:1 to stay in the EU[2], but persistently struggled to make its case to those who had not been to university. It was difficult to find anybody who campaigned for Remain, still less among the public, who could recall what its core message was. ('Britain, Stronger in Europe' was the slogan that was put up against 'Take back control'.)

When the question of immigration came up, Remain mainly tried to change the subject back to the economic risks as quickly as possible. David Cameron and Theresa May had decided in 2015 to keep their unachievable and always-missed target – to reduce net migration to under 100,000 – which was clearly impossible given EU freedom of movement if the country voted to Remain. Leave had found a much more emotionally powerful message about control, but the advocacy of Nigel Farage persistently put off as many people as it attracted. The campaign chose to duck most of the crucial questions about what would happen next if it won.

Given that both sides chose to avoid the questions that undecided voters most wanted answers to, either might have ended up on 48–49 per cent or 51–52 per cent of the referendum vote. Boris Johnson wrote two columns, to help him make his mind up, before choosing heart over head, and leading the Leave campaign. Had he jumped the other way, the knife-edge result might have gone the other way too. Given such a narrow result, just one or two shifting factors could each have made a significant difference to the outcome.

What finally decided the referendum was who turned up to vote for it, but in a way that had not been widely anticipated. The main theory about 'differential turnout' was that an unusually low turnout would be good news for Leave, since its older voting base includes many people who habitually turn out in local and European elections when most other people don't bother. They were less likely to be put off from voting for Brexit if it happened to rain on referendum day. So it was thought that a higher turnout – above 60 per cent or close to matching that for a General Election – would help Remain, who needed to bring more younger voters to the polls in particular.

The twist was that an unusually high turnout won it for Leave. If the 31 million people who had voted in the 2015 General

Election had decided this referendum too, it might have been Remain who squeezed home – by 51 per cent to 49 per cent. But three million unexpected voters turned up to the 2016 referendum, increasing turnout to 72 per cent, compared to 65 per cent for the 2015 General Election. Two-thirds of this surge in turnout chose to vote Leave.[3] Many people who had last cast a vote in 1997 or 2001, when election turnout fell sharply, believed that the choice offered in this referendum was worth taking part in. So the referendum secured a vote of confidence in the possibility of democratic participation from some who seemed to have given up on it. Leading psephologist John Curtice reported that most of those who still did not vote – with lower turnout in London and Scotland, among ethnic minorities and younger voters – leant more to Remain than Leave.

The turnout surge negated the core premise of the Remain campaign strategy. The expectation was that waverers would finally make a risk-averse choice for the status quo, given the uncertainties of voting to leave without any clear plan for Brexit. What the turnout surge showed was that the referendum had raised the stakes. Voters had perhaps intuitively understood the implicit purpose of Cameron's referendum was to settle and remove this question from British politics. Despite the unanswered questions about Brexit, one risk of voting to stay in was that people might never be asked this question again.

Why could Remain find so little to say about patriotism?

'It's the economy, stupid' was the Remain strategy. The campaign largely narrowed down to a single argument: that people could not afford to take the risk of leaving the European Union. Remain barely tried to make an argument about identity at all. In part, this was because many pro-Europeans misunderstood what their identity challenge was. It was too late, by 2016, to try to make a positive case for European identity that could resonate with a majority of people. That would have been the work of years, perhaps decades, not of the weeks or months of a short campaign. Only around 15 per cent of people had identified as European in British Social Attitudes research, even when able to choose and combine as many identities as respondents chose. European was the primary identity for 2–4 per cent of the public.[4] So the focus on practical issues and economic risks was rational for a campaign that needed to secure 50 per cent of the vote, but it left an important gap.

Yet Remain could have sought to contest the terrain of identity, history and national pride in a different way. The category error was to think that a Remain argument about identity needed to make the positive case for European identity. In fact, what was needed was something different: an argument about British pride and patriotism that saw British participation within Europe as compatible with it, rather than a threat to, what it means to be British.

The British clearly had a rather different 'psychological contract' with the European project than most of the other members. Britain had joined late, having chosen to stay out at the start, with bigger fish to fry at the top table, before being refused entry by President de Gaulle, who had explicitly cited English exceptionalism as the reason for his veto. Britain finally joined in 1973 in an era of decline, at a psychological low point. As the 1975 referendum decided whether to stay in, Sir Christopher Soames warned that 'in our present parlous condition, this is no time to consider leaving a Christmas Club, never mind the common market'.[5] By contrast, almost all of the other members gained something positive in their narratives of national identity through their engagement in the European project. For the original six, European cooperation was part of the 'never again' compact after the world wars. Our nearest neighbour, Ireland, saw in Europe a way to move out of England's shadow, reimagining itself as a more confident, younger and modernising European nation. For Spain, Portugal and Greece, Europe meant modernity and another way to entrench democracy when the dictators fell as late as the 1970s, while the central and East European countries saw the choice of EU membership as completing the dissolution of the Iron Curtain that had isolated them from the western half of the continent for almost half a century.

Finding this patriotic voice of Remain may have been challenging. But the origins story of a patriotic case for full European engagement would have been rooted in Britain's contribution to winning the Second World War. Nothing in Britain's long history makes us prouder than the blood and treasure we spent to win that peace. The prize was not just the NHS at home, but a democratic Europe abroad, if only across half of the continent at first. The emergence of the Federal Republic of Germany and the post-war democracies of Europe was a shared achievement in which Britain had a big stake. That did not mean there were no arguments inside this club of democracies. But Margaret Thatcher had not quit it; rather, she had stayed at the table and got her handbag out to secure a better deal, while championing the single market, and helping to realise Churchill's vision of melting the Iron Curtain across the continent.

There were just two glimpses of this type of argument for Remain. Former Prime Minister Gordon Brown made an effort at it, filming in the ruins of Coventry Cathedral, to blend a message of peace and patriotism. David Cameron said his 'finest hour' of the campaign was his closing 'Britain doesn't quit' peroration in the final hustings, yet this had never been a theme of his campaign. Remain had effectively conceded patriotism, history and identity to its opponents and tried to make a head over heart case for staying in anyway on the grounds of the economy alone. Nick Clegg said Britain would be 'Billy no mates' and talked about 'Great Britain, not Little England', apparently without noticing this was a pejorative reference to English identity, which tended to matter more than British identity among many swing and undecided voters. Whether or not it would have made a sufficient difference, it was a mistake for Remain not to stake its own claim to national pride and history, so that it could at least have contested the argument about identity and patriotism.

Why many ethnic minority Britons sat out the Brexit identity wars

One of the strange things about the 2016 referendum was that once this became the moment of a big, polarising argument about immigration and identity – questions that had been bubbling under for half a century – many of Britain's ethnic minorities felt like non-combatants in an argument that felt like an existential question to others. It would be difficult to underestimate the indifference of most ethnic minority Britons to the European argument that had raged for over four decades in British politics. But perhaps the indifference was reciprocal. Neither the pro-European nor the Eurosceptic political tribes had ever shown much positive interest in non-white Britain.

Some pro-Europeans seemed surprised that they could not simply assume that ethnic minorities would rally to their cause, just because of who was on the other side. Britain's pro-European movement was a case of cosmopolitanism without diversity, which is rather too common a phenomenon in progressive civic society. I doubt I would need the fingers of both hands to count the number of black and Asian Britons I have met over the years who express a strong sense of European identity. That is still often explicitly or implicitly coded as white, to a much greater extent than modern British identity is now. The European institutions were often broadly allergic to discussions of racial discrimination, and much of the thin sprinkling of ethnic diversity around the institutions in Brussels tended to be British.

Had it not been for a deep legacy of mistrust of the most prominent Eurosceptic voices in different generations – from Enoch Powell to Nigel Farage – ethnic minority Britons could easily have been natural Eurosceptics, given a much stronger sense of British than European identity; a scepticism as to whether European free movement was the fairest approach to immigration. Some campaigners for Leave recognised their own challenge of mistrust. Douglas Carswell, the pro-immigration libertarian Eurosceptic MP for Clacton, became convinced that there was a 'Farage paradox', that the most prominent pro-Leave public voice was narrowing support for Leave. Carswell's surprising conclusion was that he should himself join Farage's party, 'we have to put some men in their trench', and try to modernise UKIP or otherwise minimise its voice in the campaign.[6] I thought what Carswell was trying to do was important in seeking to somewhat lower the existential stakes of the referendum. It was an effort to persuade his fellow Leavers that they had to make the argument from and to the Britain of 2016, not the Britain of 1972. I hosted a British Future speech in which Carswell set out why the Leave campaign had to disown the legacy of Enoch Powell. Carswell argued that 'immigration has not been without its challenges. Yet it has been, overwhelmingly, a story of success. Britain today is more at ease with the multiethnic society that we have become than once seemed imaginable – and not just to Enoch Powell.'

Though Vote Leave did seek to sideline Nigel Farage, it certainly did not consistently pursue Carswell's liberal Leave argument on immigration. There was a mainstream, reasoned case for a points-based system rather than free movement, voiced by Gisela Stuart and Michael Gove. There were even some pledges of higher non-EU immigration, such as Priti Patel launching a 'save our curry houses' campaign, claiming that ending EU free movement would allow more Bangladeshi chefs to come to Britain. But alongside this, Leave pushed the immigration argument hard, putting forward the message that 'Turkey (population 76 million) is joining the EU' as one of its biggest reasons to vote Leave. The campaign warned that giving 'visa-free travel to 77 million Turkish citizens would create a border-free zone from Iraq, Iran and Syria to the English Channel'. Birmingham MP Khalid Mahmood, who had been one of the few pro-Leave Labour MPs, switched back to Remain due to the campaign messages about Turkish immigration.

By the end of the campaign, ethnic minority Britons ended up rather more likely to be reluctant Remainers, but less likely too to cast a vote in the referendum at all. Among those who took part, Remain prevailed by about two to one among Asian Britons and three to one among black Britons. This varied by social class and geography, with plenty of black and Asian votes to Leave in Birmingham, Leicester and Bradford. Ipsos-Mori estimated ethnic minority turnout to be 57 per cent of registered voters, some 17 per cent below the white British turnout of 74 per cent. (This gap was only 5 per cent in the 2017 General Election: 64 per cent to 69 per cent.) Half a million fewer ethnic minority voters took part than if there had been no ethnic participation gap in the referendum. The 2016 referendum seemed a lower-stakes event for ethnic minority Britons than a standard General Election, while white British voters on both sides of the argument tended to think that it mattered more.

I came to think that how existential the EU referendum felt as a matter of identity depended on what you thought the question on the ballot paper really meant. Was it about the United

Kingdom, in 2016, deciding whether its future lay within the EU or outside of it? Or was it about whether to turn the clock back to before 1973 – to a world of pounds, shilling and pence and a much less diverse society? Many Remainers feared the latter. The spike in post-referendum hate crime showed that the minority of Leavers who still hoped to send them all back felt legitimised by the result, though it was clear those views were a minority within the 52 per cent. Looking across the European Union, the progress that we had made on ethnic minority inclusion in my lifetime had certainly not been a shared EU-wide project in concert with France, Belgium and Italy, which had made much weaker progress on anti-discrimination and were mostly officially allergic to collecting ethnicity and race data. It was something that had happened here in Britain. We could maintain it beyond Brexit, but that would depend on how we handled the aftermath.

Why did Brexit divide us so much?

Referendums divide. This vote – 17.4 million to 16.1 million – split the country almost down the middle. The choices made illuminated much longer-standing social divisions. It divided opinion by generation, as those with a lived memory of Britain outside the European Union voted heavily to leave, while most of the under-forties were not persuaded of the case. It divided opinion by social class and above all by educational status, as three-quarters of those who had been to university voted to Remain, while most of those who had not voted to Leave.

The strangest thing about Britain's Brexit divisions was how the referendum came to divide us rather more in 2019 than it had in 2016. On referendum day, four out of ten voters on both sides reported that they had made up their minds within the final four weeks of the campaign.[7] Yet, three years later, nine out of ten people identified with the vote that they had cast in June 2016. As Maria Sobolewska and Rob Ford put it in their authoritative academic study *Brexitland*, 'Voters on both sides of the Brexit debate now had a sense of themselves as distinct social groups with their own values and priorities, and views about who their opponents were and what they stood for.'[8]

Ford and Sobolewska show how these new Brexit identities were stronger than the fading attachments to political parties. It was not just that Brexit itself felt like a 'them' and 'us' issue. The bigger danger came from how many voters began to see events, parties and policies through the lens of their new Brexit tribes.

An important consequence of this affective polarisation was that the Brexit aftermath was a story of bad winners and bad losers. Each side blamed the other for the failure of any attempt to compromise or build bridges.

A 52–48 victory was close but clear. It was a mandate to leave the European Union. Half of Remain voters believed the government had a duty to implement the result. But little effort was made by the winners to make the delivery of Brexit a shared future project. Instead, those who won the referendum often sounded as if they would be happier if they had lost it, always vigilant that Brexit would be betrayed. Maybe it was an error to choose a first post-Brexit Prime Minister, Theresa May, who had campaigned for Remain. May set out clear 'red lines' for a pretty hard Brexit, and yet was castigated as a Remainer anyway over her efforts to compromise over Northern Ireland. Though the pro-Leave camp ultimately prevailed from the political stalemate, with Boris Johnson's clear victory in the 2019 General Election, they had been less successful in normalising Brexit. Two-thirds of the public (including half of Remain voters) felt it was important to deliver on the referendum result in 2016. Six years after the referendum, 50 per cent of people felt that it had been, in retrospect, the wrong decision, while 36 per cent felt that it had been the right decision. Three-quarters of people on both sides stuck to the position that they had taken in 2016, though there was a gradual erosion of support for Brexit, not least because Leave struggled to engage across the generational divide. Eighty per cent of those too young to vote in 2016 were sceptical about Brexit and in principle favoured re-joining the EU.

Rather more was said about the bad losers. Many of those on the Remain side couldn't believe they had lost. It was surprising to see European flags and faces painted with blue and yellow stars in the weeks after the result, given that there had been so few visible expressions of European identity during the campaign, or in the decades that preceded it. Efforts to turn the 48 per cent tribe into a vibrant new political movement looked much like the early stages of a grieving process. Those who had been on the losing side spent most of that three-year stalemate period talking to themselves, rarely engaging with those late converts to Leave who they had not quite managed to persuade in the referendum itself. That was never more true than when an argument against referendums in principle was combined with a plea for just one more referendum – to put everything right after the last one – before the concept would be banished forever. This was how *The Guardian* columnist Polly Toynbee made exactly that case in 2018:

I will join the march on June 23rd [for a People's Vote] ... above all, because I think the no-Brexit position could win. But please God, let there be no other referendum ever again: never forget the near-mortal damage done to Britain by an irrevocable vote on an unfathomably complex question. Instead, trust in General Elections to throw the bastards out when they get things wrong.[9]

On several issues unconnected to the European Union – especially issues of culture and identity, like the Black Lives Matter anti-racism protests, and perceptions about where to draw the line between free speech and hate speech, the Brexit divide remained a significant predictor, mainly due to the underlying divisions by age and education, by geography and by politics, which shaped people's choices for Remain and Leave.

What had it all been for? There were clearly economic costs of Brexit, arising from the increased friction in the trade rules with the European Union, though the impact of the Covid pandemic and the energy crisis made it easier for partisan opponents to disagree about what could be attributed to Brexit. Had there been any benefits? Remainers felt it was increasingly clear there were none that justified the pain. The referendum had a cathartic effect in showing that democratic choices could make a difference. Changing to a new immigration system contributed to a softening and warming of attitudes, even as immigration numbers stayed high. There was much more attention paid to geographical inequality in Britain. This was a domestic shift, a by-product of the referendum campaign. The government department for communities and local government was renamed to focus on 'Levelling Up'. How far that turns into a substantive agenda remains to be seen.

The referendum divide could have been handled much better, though opinions were predictably polarised on who bore most responsibility for the failure. Had a more effective Remain campaign, perhaps by being that little bit more patriotic, sneaked a narrow victory of 52 per cent of the vote, arguably this might have delivered a wake-up call to the political classes about democratic dissatisfaction and geographical inequality, without the many practical difficulties of having to deliver Brexit itself. (Though there would doubtless have been a different campaign for a second referendum, for example, from Nigel Farage's Brexit

Party in the 2019 European elections.) Alternatively, what if the narrow Leave victory had been followed by a government led by prominent Leavers like Boris Johnson and Michael Gove, in 2016 rather than 2019? There would have been a quicker, unilateral decision to protect the rights of EU nationals in Britain than Theresa May was prepared to offer, which might not only have reassured over three million European nationals in the UK, but perhaps have changed the mood music too. But it is less clear whether such a government could have sought to reach across the Brexit divide, or have succeeded if it had done so.

Neither of those paths was followed. So British politics was rarely as angry as it became during the Brexit stand-off of 2016 to 2019. The Brexit tribes had never been stronger while the question of Brexit remained unresolved. The European elections of 2019 saw a brief meltdown of the party system, as the Brexit Party and the Liberal Democrats effectively became the Leave and Remain parties. After three years of stalemate, the referendum winners won again in the 2019 General Election. Those campaigning for a second referendum had missed the simple power of Sam's point: the need to do what people had voted for first. But if Leave had much the better of the stalemate years from 2016 to 2019, it struggled with what to do next once it had won again in 2019. The post-2020 challenge has been to show what Brexit can deliver. If the pro-Brexit argument merely defaults to claiming that Brexit has been betrayed, or has never been tried, this is likely to appeal only to a shrinking core, especially by the time of the tenth anniversary of the 2016 referendum in 2026.

Britain's departure from the European Union on 30 January 2020 did not end the argument about Britain's relationships in Europe. But it significantly reduced the intensity of Brexit polarisation. The Covid pandemic saw a broad consensus on the initial lockdown, for the furlough scheme and the vaccine rollout. Even anger at parties in Downing Street reached across party and referendum divides, leading to Boris Johnson's departure last summer. There was disappointment in Billericay at the ousting of Boris Johnson, despite disapproval of the Downing Street parties. Due to the 'back-stabbing and infighting' in Westminster, both Sam and Kathy wondered if they would bother voting for anybody next time, feeling that it was time for a change.

That the Truss government suffered such a significant reputational damage from its first major policy initiative on taking office – its mini-budget, which sought to cut taxes at the very top – also demonstrated a weakening of Brexit affiliations. A significant portion of the 2019 swing voters chose to switch parties again over this economic issue, in a larger short-term swing than over the ERM crisis, or for any recently elected Prime Minister in the post-war period.

The dominant public mood over Brexit is often now one of exhaustion. That was felt even in Billericay. Sam said he would be happy to never hear another word about Brexit again, even wondering if he would have voted for it had he known it would go on for so long.

The Sunak–Starmer era of British politics might start to reflect that Brexit fatigue. Sunak's Windsor Castle renegotiation of the Northern Irish protocol demonstrated that pragmatic cooperation between post-Brexit Britain and its European neighbours could sometimes exceed expectations. Could it become Keir Starmer's political project to save Brexit? That is now the logic of his political project, if that was not a role the Labour leader would have imagined trying to play when he entered parliament in 2015, nor perhaps even in 2017 either. If Labour does come to power at the next General Election, it will be the first time that the referendum 'losers' get to grapple with Brexit in power. So a hypothetical Labour government would have the opportunity to play a bridging role, having been elected mainly (but not entirely) with the votes of those who think the idea is quixotic.

I think it is a strong common-sense principle that a decision made by a referendum can only be undone by a future referendum. Therefore, Labour's policy is to 'Make Brexit Work' and part of Starmer's challenge is to communicate that to sceptical swing voters. The best way to do so would be for a Labour government, on coming to power, to attempt what was not tried in 2016 and 2019: to hold the broadest possible engagement, with stakeholders and the public, on how to make Brexit work: on what has worked well, what problems have arisen, and what the potential solutions to them are, so as to inform the British government's approach to the UK–EU review of the Brexit deal. All this is likely to be combined with the insight that making Brexit work can and should involve more practical cooperation with our friends across the Channel –with the EU. This may help to assuage the disappointment of some ex-Remainers who may, at heart, still be re-joiners but for whom the shape of Brexit could make a difference. Could this be a route to a new post-Brexit equilibrium, as the deal is renewed, or will there be an ongoing partisan tug-of-war between softer and harder Brexits?

There may be growing political pressure inside the Labour Party to put the single market, which Conservatives would want to rule out, back on the agenda by the second half of the decade. The challenge for re-joiners is to try to persuade one of the major parties, more likely Labour, to make a referendum pledge in 2029, 2033, 2037, 2041 or later. What the architecture of the European Union and the wider continent would be in future decades may change the question again, but even some of those who regret the first result may take a lot of persuading about the value of inviting us all to revisit the question.

It was good that we had kept talking about Brexit in Billericay, in the margins of family birthdays and major sporting events.

The in-laws were happy for me to transmit occasional bulletins for Billericay on social media too for the benefit of the Westminster crowd: 'Let them know how we, the people, see it,' said Sam. Even if it was only one-half of the argument, it was important to keep talking across the Brexit divides.

8

Mixed Up

**Could our blurred boundaries one day
take us beyond race?**

Britain is becoming more ethnically diverse – decade on decade. Yet the Katwala household in Dartford turns out to be bucking the trend. We reported in the 2021 census that we had become considerably less 'ethnically diverse' during the decade just gone. When there were five of us in 2011, the Office of National Statistics were told that four-fifths of our household were ethnic minority citizens. By 2021, the family size had grown by one, yet we had somehow also now become two-thirds white British in these official ethnicity statistics.

In filling in the form, as a parent, just over a decade ago, I had ascribed to a five-year-old, a four-year-old and a two-year-old a similar ethnic identity to my own: 'mixed race: white and Asian'. What had changed, by census day in March 2021, was that it had become possible to ask those children – now 15, 14 and 12 – what answers they would give for themselves. As we gathered around my laptop to consider the options, the three that I had officially categorised as mixed race now chose 'white British' as their ethnic identity. (The 16-year-old also adopted an additional national identity – Irish – signalling that, with an Irish-born grandmother on both sides, she may decide to take up her right to Irish citizenship by descent, either as a symbolic gesture or for its potential practical benefits in a post-Brexit world.)

Their nine-year-old sister, not born until after the 2011 census, was the other 'mixed ethnicity' member of the household this time around. She did not have any strong preference about what to choose. So I suspect that this may have been largely a sympathy vote, seeing that nobody else was choosing to stay in Dad's team this time around. If the government did conduct another census in a decade, it may well be that the ethnic group identity she holds at nineteen may not be the same one that we just officially recorded for her at age nine.

There was no doubt at all that what would go on the form would reflect the children's own preferences. I am a long-standing believer in a liberal principle of personal autonomy when it comes to people's sense of ethnic identity: people should decide for themselves whichever labels they think best describe their own sense of identity and heritage, and it is a good thing for other people try to follow and reflect that where feasible. Yet I found myself a little bit surprised about the choices they had made. Maybe I had somewhat *mixed* feelings about this move away from recognising or identifying with their mixed ethnic heritage.

After all, we, the mixed-race population, had moved on and moved up. We were no longer this marginal, mixed-up complicated footnote, being neither one thing nor the other, the source of irreconcilable anxieties and heartache about identity.[1] From being a social problem, we had become a fashionable solution: the bridgers in polarised times. Weren't we the proof that at least *somebody* was integrating? Indeed, with so many relationships across ethnic lines, we were now said to be the trend-setters. Once official recognition was granted, we were now the fastest-growing group of all in the census statistics. Indeed, it was sometimes suggested that we heralded a melting-pot future, where Britain would not just be 'minority-majority' by 2050, but *majority-mixed* by the end of the century, where this increasingly brown and yet somewhat beige future so blurred the boundaries between groups that people might struggle to remember what all of those arguments about race had ever been about.[2]

Well, *that* had seemed to be the plan anyway. Yet now the Katwala children were leaving all that behind, declining to play their allotted role in the *narrative* of how Britain could leave racial conflict in the past. Maybe we could still cling on to being the fastest-growing group of all when the census statistics came out, but we would be at least three votes down in Dartford. The children were moving on, moving out, maybe even moving up as they migrated over into the majority group, declining to play their allotted role in this narrative of how racial conflict could be left in the past. I didn't say any of that to them, of course.

Newspaper headlines do often declare that Britain will be 'minority-majority' by 2070, yet these census choices of the Katwala children show why some of those projections should be taken with a grain of salt. Those linear graphs may be relying on the Katwala children, and perhaps their hypothetical future children too, to keep contributing to the accelerating ethnic diversity of Britain when they have ceased to pull their weight in that direction. Demographers know many things when they make estimates and projections, but what they do not know is how those people represented on the graphs will think about their own identity half a century from now. The boxes that my children ticked capture emerging nuances – that the rise of ethnic diversity would be a little more gradual than graphs showing exponential growth may predict – but this would partly reflect that the white majority group itself had become a little bit more ethnically mixed. An important part of the future British story of diversity and integration is that the statistical categories will come under increasing pressure from the complex lived experience of real life.

So can I choose too?

I could have seen this coming. One of the first conversations I recall about the children's sense of ethnic identity happened shortly after the death of Nelson Mandela, which was just before my eldest daughter's seventh birthday. The primary school held an assembly about his life, and so she was explaining to me what she had heard about the system of apartheid in South Africa: under those rules, she said, she would not have been allowed to be in the same class as her friends. She mentioned a friend in her class who was black to exemplify that. So I wondered which class she might be in herself. 'Maybe we are mixed,' said her five-year-old brother, mentioning the blue spot birthmark on his chin, since he had been told this was more common for children who had parents from different ethnic backgrounds. Obviously, any attempt to work out whether they might find themselves in the white, black or mixed-race classroom certainly reinforced the assembly's message that racial apartheid was a very bad idea, compared to their own school. Yet the children could tell that the boundaries were blurred and so they could, they decided, choose which group they were part of. I thought that was really interesting. Lots of people might think they didn't have that choice, I said. They might feel their ethnicity was something that was decided for them. Maybe their ability to choose and decide for themselves might be an advantage of coming from a mix of different backgrounds.

I also asked them if I could choose too: could I decide I was Indian, like my dad, or white, like my mum, or mixed race? But my primary-school jury felt that I might now be trying to stretch the flexibility too far. The not-quite-seven-year-old asked me to give her my arm, and she put it next to her own. 'Sorry, Dad, but I don't think you can choose as well. Your arm is a bit too dark. I think you're definitely mixed race,' she told me.

A decade later, my sixteen-year-old is not entirely convinced of the value of my sharing this particular anthropological anecdote about how primary-school children start to think about race. But we did talk about that conversation again, several years later, when we were discussing the impact of the Black Lives Matter protests of 2020. She approached those anti-racism protests in a spirit of supportive allyship. Her reasoning is that race is often a social issue of how other people perceive you. 'If most people treat you as if you have white privilege, most of the time, then you do have white privilege,' she says. 'I don't really buy this idea if somebody can say, well I am one-sixteenth Caribbean, so I am going to identify as Black.' Even if that might not apply when somebody is looking at the name on her CV when she applies for a job. As we were talking about some of the ways in which people think and talk about race have changed, I told her about the concepts of 'black unity' and 'political blackness' that had been widespread in the 1970s and 1980s. She found the idea that not only I might identify as Black, but she could too, to be fairly incomprehensible.

'What's all of this mixed-race nonsense?'

'Mixed race? What's all of this mixed-race nonsense? If you're not white, you're black' was how the late Darcus Howe put this old point to me, when we were about to discuss a particular race twitterstorm in a teacup in a panel discussion at *Newsnight*.[3] Howe was a major figure in British race relations, his role in the

Mangrove trial now immortalised in Steve McQueen's film. He had also been an early adopter, in his groundbreaking *White Tribe* series for Channel 4, of the idea that race equality needed to think about the majority identity too. But it did still feel a bit retro to be having this old argument put to me as late as 2012.

I have never identified as white but I had never considered myself black either. That might simply have been a generational thing. Had I gone to university in the 1970s rather than the 1990s then I might have done so. As it was, I doubt I was particularly aware of this invitation or offer, this expansive concept of blackness, until I got to university. The adjectives and labels that I associated myself with were fairly well established by then. I think it would definitely have felt like I was trying too hard if I had decided to come out as black in the early 1990s. I imagine that the intellectual argument would have made some sense to a few people in the student union and the university Labour Club but it would have been greeted with some bemusement by most of my contemporaries beyond that. This may be why that expansive sense of 'black' in its broader 1970s umbrella sense of black and Asian unity would increasingly be described as 'political blackness', accurately capturing how this had become a concept promoted among the active and highly engaged, largely for its strategic benefits as a coalition-building theory of civic and political change for ethnic minorities, rather than as a reflection of how people or groups tended to think about ethnic identity. Professor Tariq Modood had shown by the early 1990s that most British Asians did not identify as 'black', despite the 1980s hegemony of 'political blackness' in the academy, though a sizeable minority of around a third did so.[4]

A lack of interest in this 'mixed-race nonsense' was, however, shared by the Office of National Statistics when they first began to collect ethnicity data. It was remarkably late in the last century, as recently as 1991, that race and ethnicity first made it into the census, after preparations to include it in 1981 were abandoned, from a mixture of uncertainty about exactly how to ask the question in a way that was legitimate, perhaps combined with a variety of political anxieties about what people might think of either the principle or the results.

There was no 'mixed race' category the first time around. That was not an oversight, but a conscious omission. For some reason, the official hunch was that most people with mixed ethnic heritage would probably still want to pick one group, so the official guidance invited such respondents to 'select the ethnic group with which they identify'. The initial 1991 options were White, Black-Caribbean, Black-African, Black-Other, Indian, Pakistani, Bangladeshi and Chinese, though 'any other ethnic group' was available for those omitted from that list, as well as being a not entirely satisfactory alternative pigeonhole for us mixed-race oddities. By 2001, feedback about those choices had changed official minds, so there was not only a new 'mixed race' category, but some interest too in what might be going on within it, with four sub-categories: White and Black Caribbean, White and Black African, White and Asian, and 'Any Other Mixed Background'. No doubt some of us will insist on remaining a bit too complicated for these forms, however many options are added. The British census understands that there is a white Irish group, but the idea that anybody might have any need or use of a mixed-race Irish category had not occurred to the census-designers of England and Wales, with the mixed-race Indian-Irish even further off the radar (though black Irish, Asian Irish, and mixed-race Irish did begin to feature in the Irish census from 2006).

Mixed ethnicity has been the fastest-growing ethnic group of the last two decades in Britain, and is likely to become the biggest single minority group in the next one. But generalisations about the mixed-race population are complicated by the increasing fluidity of race and ethnic identification among the mixed-race group in particular. The research of Lucinda Platt and Alita Nandi suggests that the number of people with mixed ethnic heritage may be about to *triple* the number who tick that box on the census form. Among children whose parents were from different ethnic groups, about a third identified themselves as 'white British', a similar proportion to the third who identified as 'mixed race', while another third had a range of other minority identities, such as black, Asian and so on.

This voluntary assimilation into the white British group over a generation or two had long been a common feature among those from European backgrounds – those with Hungarian or Polish parents, for example. In 2011, only around one in seven British-born children with an Irish parent gave their ethnic identity as 'Irish', despite a 'tick the Irish box' campaign to encourage those of Irish descent to do so. Irish identity in Britain seems to work differently from Irish identity in the United States of America, where Joe Biden has maintained a strongly Irish-American identification in the [eighth] generation, to a considerably greater extent than my children do, though their direct ancestral connections to Ireland are intact a century later than his.

That something similar would also happen, over time, with visible minority groups was perhaps more surprising – though the Black Caribbean group's exceptionally high level of inter-ethnic relationships made it an early trend-setter that other groups may emulate over time. When he is asked about the origins of his surname at school, my 15-year-old son tells me he says 'my dad is half-Indian' rather than 'I am a quarter-Indian'. He is sceptical about the mixed-race and ethnic minority total-iser trying to cover everybody with an ethnic minority: 'Wasn't that one-grandparent rule what Hitler was trying to do with his Nuremberg Laws?' he asks me. So race in Britain is becoming more flexible. Or is it?

Two cheers for Black Lives Matter

Had I taken up Darcus Howe's offer – to pick a side, and identify as 'black' or 'white' – I might have been politely asked to desist from staking a claim to black identity within the decade.

A little-noticed feature of the Black Lives Matter anti-racism protests of 2020 was how they quietly drew to a close what had once been the hegemonic civic society articulation of blackness – as an anti-racist umbrella identity for British ethnic minorities. British Asians had been increasingly sceptical about this from the 1990s and the black British used this seminal 2020s moment, which was reshaping the civic conversation about race, to move on from it too.

When the killing of George Floyd took place, I heard and read enough about those nine minutes of footage to decide that I did not need to watch his death myself. The anger in America was immediate and palpable. That message crossed the Atlantic too: first, to express solidarity with the tragedy in America, and then to raise issues of race and injustice in Britain. The early stages of the Covid pandemic had highlighted stark ethnic inequalities of life and death. Over 150 NHS staff had lost their lives in the first three months of the pandemic: a tragically high proportion – two-thirds – from ethnic minority backgrounds.[5]

Covid made me ambivalent about the decision to hold Black Lives Matter protests in Britain. Placards declaring 'racism is the real pandemic' risked mixing metaphors to deadly effect. The Covid context was one more feature making this an inter-ethnic movement largely of the young – black, white and Asian – though many older black and Asian Britons were glad to be armchair supporters. Almost a third of ethnic minority Britons reported that they felt they had played some part in the protest movement, mostly by voicing support online.[6] And most people

– ethnic minority and white Britons – said that they had talked about the anti-racism protests with friends and family, colleagues and others. I spent a lot of that summer and autumn talking to people about what the protests had meant to them.[7]

The anti-racism protests meant many different things to different people. They were as much a spontaneous response as a coordinated effort. The Black Lives Matter movement, active in the US since 2016, had no formal association with those adopting the movement in the UK. Most local activities were independently organised. There was no coordinated manifesto or action plan. Most of ethnic minority Britain thought the protests mattered: two-thirds said they were supportive of them, rising to eight out of ten of the black British.[8] That is an impressive proportion, when you consider that the black British make up less than a quarter of the non-white visible minority population of the UK. Anti-black prejudice has been too common among British Asian communities, and this is one hopeful sign that it is declining across generations. Half of the white majority population were supportive of the protests, while a quarter said they were opposed to them: education, age and politics were significant factors, with much higher levels of support among young people, graduates and those who lean left politically than among older people and those with conservative views.

There were, broadly, five different views of the Black Lives Matter protests.

For strong supporters, they were an urgent long-overdue wake-up call for action. The specific recognition of anti-black prejudice was a key element for the strongest supporters – about a quarter of the population, about a third of ethnic minorities, and a majority of black Britons. Strong supporters could sometimes be more pessimistic than others about whether the protests would lead to more than tokenistic change from powerful institutions.

Moderate supporters saw the protests as bringing new energy to anti-racism, which needed to move from talk to action, though they had some concerns about an increasingly polarised debate about race. This segment – a third of ethnic minorities and a quarter of the white population – tended to see the protests as having a broad anti-racism message, about the need for an agenda to tackle racism and discrimination against all groups.

About a quarter of both white and ethnic minority Britons identified themselves as on the fence about the protests, neither for nor against. The main source of ambivalence was, initially, especially about the timing during lockdown, while public caution about Covid meant support for restrictions remained high. This segment combined sympathy for George Floyd with questions about why a tragedy in America had sparked protests in Britain too. Yet those who described themselves as on the fence were at pains to emphasise their commitment to anti-racism, often focusing on hate crime and racism online, being both less familiar with and less persuaded by arguments about institutional racism.

The mainstream opponents of the protests were social conservatives who focused on the arguments about statues as exemplifying why bringing America's race politics to Britain would do more to divide than unite. More political arguments – that the protests naively endorsed critical race theory, cultural Marxism or calls to defund the police – were less common than in online debate. Nor did those arguments reflect what those who took part thought the protests meant to them.

The toxic critics comprised up to a tenth of the population, and their opposition was clearly driven by latent racial resentment and overt prejudice.[9] This group had a higher profile online, which also influenced how supporters of the protests perceived their opponents. Almost everybody who engaged with the protests online had come across racist opposition to them.

Among those five broad views of the protests, four of them had significant points, worth taking seriously. And there was more give and take between them away from heated online exchanges. Quite a lot of people wanted to be in listening mode that summer. Many people were interested in what their colleagues from minority backgrounds made of the protests, albeit likely to let them raise the subject first, if they wanted to. Young people, from conversations at home, were aware that different generations often saw the protests differently. That Britain wasn't America on race turned out to be common ground. Supporters of the protests were quick to recognise that America's problem with guns made its issues with race and policing of a different scale and intensity, though they were also concerned that too much focus on the transatlantic differences could slip into complacency about the real challenges that Britain had to face up to.

Has change on race in Britain been fast or slow? That question gets to the heart of how we talk past each other on race, because the social changes of the last few decades have felt both dizzyingly fast and frustratingly slow at the same time.

I could understand why it felt discombobulating for older white Britons to face a much more assertive anti-racist challenge in the 2020s, having seen a rapid acceleration of ethnic diversity in their adult lifetimes, and feeling that they, and their country, had done a good deal to adjust to it, from realising that some of the old 'banter' did not feel like a joke to those on the receiving end, to passing anti-discrimination laws, and seeing a growing number of Asian and black voices in the media, politics and senior positions of work. It didn't seem fair to claim that little or nothing had changed.

Yet that does not negate the young black British perspective that the journey to equal opportunities remains frustratingly slow. Young adults, born in this century, are not going to feel grateful to hear of the decline of 1970s 'Paki-bashing' by National Front thugs, or of the monkey chanting that I used to hear at football. The UK has a good case to be a comparative leader in the efforts we make on race equality, but the countries of western Europe have hardly set a high bar, when the philosophical allergy to collecting ethnic data makes conducting the types of race audit that are becoming routine in the UK impossible.

To insist on a comparative lens (whether across time or across countries) can be a tone-deaf response to the call for change to speed up. For younger Britons, the test is whether they have equal opportunity now, not whether their opportunities and horizons have expanded since their grandparents' generation stepped off the *Windrush* three-quarters of a century ago. If you are worried about fair chances when sending in a CV with an identifiably ethnic minority name in Birmingham and Manchester, and the evidence still shows you will need to send in 60 per cent more CVs to secure the same number of interviews, it is hardly going to be relevant to be told you might face more discrimination still in Brussels or Marseilles. Indeed, that rather conveys the 'them and us' premise that young ethnic minority Britons might be on some kind of mystery shopping tour to decide which country to be a minority in.

So the anti-racism protests captured why most black and Asian Britons feel there is much further to travel on an unfinished journey towards fair chances. They galvanised and cut through, but they polarised too. Just when the reality of race and opportunity in Britain has never been more complex – not just across ethnic groups, but by age, education, geography and gender within them – the public and political conversation was becoming more binary. This contrast was reflected in the extraordinary level of polarisation in the debate about the Sewell Report in the spring of 2021. Both the Government and its critics embarked on mutual recriminations over the perceived bad faith of their political opponents: either that the government is in denial about the existence of racism and discrimination in Britain, or that its critics are blind to the progress that has been made over the years.

The Sewell Commission was created as a response to the anti-racism protests, but it largely talks past those who took part in them. It does offer some faint praise for those who participated – 'we owe the many young people behind that movement a debt of gratitude for focusing our attention once again on these issues' – but its primary message is that they have misperceived the extent of change on race in Britain, arguing that 'you do not pass on the baton of progress by cleaving to a fatalistic account that insists nothing has changed'.[10] That proved an unsuccessful way to seek to bridge either generational or political divides on race. Yet the core message of the protests had been the need to speed up change in Britain.

That case for going further and faster could have been an argument that the Sewell Commission accepted and endorsed, and sought to reconcile with its own perspective: that it could build further on the progress of the past, rather than taking an excessively pessimistic view that almost nothing had changed. This would have allowed it to place more attention on the areas – the persistent ethnic disparities in recruitment despite progress in education; the trust and confidence gaps in policing; the need to tackle health disparities, and to reflect the making of modern Britain properly on the curriculum – where its substantive analysis was on the side of those seeking faster change.

It is too early to say how much difference the anti-racism protests made. The most commonly reported change is that more is happening in workplaces. Organisations with a largely graduate workforce feel under more pressure to show that their equality and diversity strategies can deliver progress on race. In major companies, there has been an acceleration of progress in the boardroom. Five years ago, most FTSE 100 boardrooms were all white, but all-white boardrooms, now down to 3 per cent, should become a thing of the past this year, with the FTSE 250 on track to meet its own voluntary target to emulate this by 2024. The charity sector lags embarrassingly behind both the public and private sector on the recruitment, retention and progression of ethnic minorities. There is a danger of more talk, more agonised 'difficult conversations' about diversity deficits, without action, through clearer analysis of the causes and timetabled plans to address them.

The new politics of anti-racism has made more positive impacts in practice, but may struggle more in theory.

Re-essentialising race? What the new politics of race gets wrong

The last 75 years should give us good insights into how to make progress on race – reducing discrimination and prejudice, and extending opportunity and equal citizenship. Social contact matters, especially when it is meaningful, and takes place in conditions of relative equality. At a societal level, shared identities underpinning our shared citizenship matter. A belief that we are all part of the 'in group', through our shared citizenship across ethnic lines, will help to maintain our willingness to fund shared institutions, such as public services and the welfare state, and to tackle discrimination, not just against members of our own group, but for everybody else too.

If the experience of recent decades shows that we make progress on race when we reduce the social distance between members of ethnic groups and increase the sense of solidarity across them, we should be wary of the risks of the new anti-racism re-essentialising race. It is legitimate to challenge notions of colour-blindness if that perspective makes organisations insufficiently interested in exploring and tackling the barriers to equal opportunities that remain. But it is quite another thing to see increasing the sense of distance between ethnic groups as a goal in itself. Anti-racism in America, especially white liberal progressive anti-racism, risks taking an essentially segregationist turn that British anti-racism should actively reject.

Fortunately, there are good reasons to expect that the new anti-racism will take a different form in Britain than America, because inter-ethnic relationships are different here. The basic demographic facts – while black Americans make up 13 per cent of the population, the black British are a 4 per cent group – interact with a different history, geography and patterns of education and social life to mean there is less social distance between black and white Britain than between black and white America.

Geography matters too. Half of the black British live in Greater London and half outside of it. So there is a significant difference in the familiarity of everyday social contact in the capital, where black people make up a sixth of the overall population, and contact in the rest of the UK, outside the major cities, where the black British are closer to one-fiftieth of the population. For many people, contact is indirect. If the black British are more familiar from news and politics, television, culture and sport than from real-life contact, then cultural and media representations, whether negative or positive, will have a bigger impact on perceptions.

Overall, there is considerably less residential and educational segregation by race in Britain than America: the main centres of black British population are either mixed areas with no single majority group, as in most inner London boroughs, or are mixed areas that are majority white. And there are much higher levels of inter-ethnic relationships – British-born people of black

Caribbean heritage are four times as likely as their American counterparts to have a white partner. These are both a consequence and a further driver of this difference.

In defence of cultural appropriation

One happy consequence of this is to considerably narrow the market in the UK for arguments about 'cultural appropriation' with its siloed and essentially segregationist implications. Take the crazy, trivial episode of Adele's hair. With the Notting Hill Carnival of 2020 able to take place only remotely, due to Covid, the pop star Adele tweeted from her Beverly Hills home, wearing a Jamaican flag bikini and with her hair in Bantu knots, that she would be happy to be at Carnival in her 'beloved London'. An American journalist, Ernest Owens, editor-in-large of *Philadelphia Magazine*, tweeted his objection to this as 'cultural appropriation', generating a mostly critical response that he had entirely missed the meaning of the London carnival. David Lammy, the black British MP for Tottenham, thought that the 'humbug' totally missed the spirit of Notting Hill Carnival. Adele, 'born and raised in Tottenham', gets it more than most. Media reports conveyed that British Jamaican opinion, from music stars like *The X Factor* winner Alexandra Burke to Popcaan, was largely positive. Author Candice Carty-Williams posted that 'Adele is an honorary Jamaican and always has been.'

Media outlets reporting the 'controversy' faced the problem that there appeared to be next to nobody in Britain, Jamaican or not, who objected. Somehow Owens, from Philadelphia, did a full broadcast media round across numerous British outlets – on LBC, Talk Radio, the BBC – keen to report this 'controversy' that next to nobody in Britain seemed to think was controversial at all. The overwhelming majority of social media responses from

Britain and Jamaica were critical of the criticism, questioning whether the world wanted America to 'be the world's cultural appropriation policeman'. Adele, having reflected on the online arguments, felt that she should apologise: 'I didn't read the room,' she said. Her willingness to engage with criticism was praised by those with different views, though the apology seemed unnecessary to me.

If you are mixed race, it becomes especially impossible to work out how the so-called rules of cultural appropriation would apply. Could I have been engaging in 'cultural appropriation' when I took Irish dancing lessons, or am I protected by my parentage in exploring my own culture, while an English class-mate who wanted to respect Irish culture could do that best by staying away? I have been told – by committed, self-identifying fascists, citing the UN declaration on the rights of indigenous peoples – that it is 'cultural appropriation' that I consider myself English. This is nonsense, but it is the type of nonsense that arguments about cultural appropriation risk legitimising.

At heart, the cultural appropriation concept depends on a set of ethno-nationalist premises: that there are fixed groups, with ownership over cultural properties, and it is theft for others to engage with or profit from these. If the issue is the 'unauthorised' use of cultural property, somebody would need to have the power to both veto and accept. This would require a level of internal consensus within a minority group that simply does not exist, and it would anyway be a form of illiberal tyranny to police individual expression, from within or beyond the group.

I have never seen any coherent account of how 'cultural appropriation' boundaries or rules could work that would not have many regressive implications. *Encyclopaedia Britannica*'s entry on cultural appropriation offers Madonna's *Vogue* video as its main example. Although Madonna 'ostensibly' respected the dance's origins, by including drag performers in her video, the profits of her double platinum album lead to the verdict that 'her use of the dance is cultural appropriation'. A common feature of essays and blogs on the topic is that these invariably assert that 'there is a fine line between appreciation and appropriation' before setting out ill-defined and subjective prohibitions that make it ultimately impossible to stay on the right side of the line.

The history of culture is the history of cultural exchange. That traditional liberal view should be defended. Instead, progressive America appears to be constructing taboos about inter-ethnic contact and exchange that bear little reality to the views taken around the world. When Hungarian President Viktor Orbán talked about being against mixed-race relationships, there was an outcry. The concept of 'cultural appropriation' is an unwitting form of progressive Orbánism. Take the logic of 'cultural appropriation' seriously, and it is difficult to see what prevents it extending to an objection to inter-ethnic adoption, and inter-ethnic relationships.

A century ago, George Bernard Shaw, considering the test of an equal society, chose marriage – or rather 'intermarriageability'.[11] A society in which there were no social objections to any marriage would be classless. The object, therefore, of social policy should be 'to keep the entire community intermarriageable'. He extended the concept to race and discrimination too. 'Marriages of White and Black: Startling Plan by Mr Shaw' screamed a *Telegraph* headline reporting Shaw's South African tour of 1931 where he argued that intermarriage would end racial tension, without persuading his audiences entirely.[12]

Shaw anticipated the sociologist's focus on intermarriage as the gold standard of integration. It is not the only thing that matters. Over the last half-century, the link between cultural integration and economic opportunity has been weaker than Shaw might have expected. Indeed, groups that have advanced most in socio-economic terms – British Chinese and British

Indians – have not matched the inter-ethnic relationships of the Black Caribbean group, which has faced persistent socio-economic disadvantage, despite the pace of social and cultural integration.

It is an important fact about our society that one in ten relationships cross ethnic lines but the growth of the mixed-race group was never the solution in itself. The mixed-race bridgers won't be able to put the country back together if everybody else still prefers their own groups and tribes. What really matters is the quality of social relationships across and between ethnic groups.

So do please tick whatever box feels right to you – but majority, minority or mixed, we can all play our part in that.

9

Opportunity Knocks

What did the rise of Rishi Sunak tell
us about Britain?

Rishi Sunak entering Downing Street as Prime Minister generated distinct responses across three different generations of the
Katwala family.

My dad felt it was a moment of profound historic significance,
and a source of pride for many British Indians, whatever their
political views or party preferences. There could be few more
powerful symbols than a British Indian Prime Minister of just
how much had changed across the five decades since Dad had
arrived in a country where the public argument about
Commonwealth migrants was whether to let some in or send
them all back. This was not something he would have thought
possible until the last two or three years.

My twin sister also saw Sunak's arrival in Downing Street as a
positive symbol of social progress, whatever his educational and
social privileges. It helped that the new Prime Minister seemed
to her more competent and trustworthy than either Liz Truss or
Boris Johnson. But she felt cooler about the new Prime Minister
within a month or two. His response to the nurses' strike didn't

suggest that he sufficiently valued the work of her NHS co-workers.

The Katwala children were much less impressed by the idea that we were witnessing some remarkable social breakthrough. What surprised them was not that the new Prime Minister was Asian but to hear that Britain had never yet had a single black or Asian Prime Minister before. 'Barack Obama was President of America quite a while ago,' my ten-year-old daughter observed. The children wondered why Britain seemed to be behind the curve on this. The teenagers had heard that Sunak had gone to a top private school and was the richest MP in parliament. That he could become Prime Minister hardly seemed much of a proof that the top roles were open to everyone.

It made sense to me that different generations might see the significance of the moment differently. When Rishi Sunak was born, in Southampton in 1980, there were no black or Asian MPs at all. You could find a few in the history books, way back in the 1890s or 1920s, but there was nobody at all for four decades after post-war immigration turned race relations into a major public issue. That began to change after 1987 but ever so gradually. When I had cast my own first vote as an adult, there were six non-white MPs, three black and three Asian, out of six hundred and fifty. But when Rishi Sunak did an internship at Conservative Central Office before graduating in 2001, every MP representing his party was white.

I had spoken with Sunak about ethnic diversity in politics in a Radio 4 discussion in May 2014, a year before he became an MP.[1] Having made some money in finance, the thirty-something Sunak was having a sort of gap year as a think-tanker at Policy Exchange, researching the growing impact of Britain's ethnic diversity.[2] Sajid Javid had just been appointed Culture Secretary that spring. It seems surprising now to realise that this, in 2014, was the very first time a British Asian MP had sat in Cabinet as

Secretary of State, given how much ethnic diversity at the top table has become commonplace since. The young Sunak said that this advance felt like an important 'turning point' for the Conservative Party, which was becoming increasingly diverse under David Cameron's leadership. He would go on to be selected as a parliamentary candidate himself a few months later. Who can say whether he imagined he might become Prime Minister within the decade?

Britain's 'no big deal' moment of social history

Sunak's accession to the premiership proved a strikingly under-stated moment of British social history. The circumstances were unusual. There had not been a General Election, nor even a party leadership election. Mid-term changes of leadership are as much the norm as the exception in our parliamentary system. Only three of the last ten Prime Ministers to take office since 1979 – Thatcher, Blair and Cameron – arrived in Downing Street after a General Election. What made the crazy political volatility of 2022 unprecedented was changing Prime Ministers twice in one parliament. After it had all gone so wrong so quickly for Liz Truss, the man who had recently lost a party leadership vote was nominated unopposed by Conservative MPs to replace the shortest-serving Prime Minister of all time.

The unlikely claim that this felt like Britain's 'Obama moment' was made by Sanjay Chandarana, president of the Southampton Vedic Society Hindu Temple. This was founded by Sunak's grandfather in 1971,[3] so Chandarana might be excused this slightly hyperbolic suggestion, which reflected a micro-climate of strong local pride among his congregation, where Sunak had posed for over a hundred photographs and selfies on his most recent visit to the temple. There could hardly have been a starker contrast between the national optics of the two occasions. On the night of Obama's election victory, the American president elect had spoken to a crowd estimated at a quarter of a million crammed into a Chicago Park. Obama quoted Abraham Lincoln, Martin Luther King Jr and JFK, and spoke of the 'arc of history' and how a change 'which had been a long time coming' had come to America, placing his election in the story of America's civil rights on a night of soaring rhetoric and sweeping emotion.

Rishi Sunak walked into Downing Steet alone, having given a short workmanlike speech about the sense of responsibility he felt in getting straight to work for the British people. There was not any direct reference to his ethnicity or faith, nor any allusion to what this meant to him or said about Britain. He was just a former Chancellor, pledging to fix the mistakes and set to work trying to get things back on track. The very British approach to an 'Obama moment' was to not mention it at all.

Rishi Sunak's political opponents were warm about what his premiership symbolised. Labour leader Keir Starmer congratulated the new Prime Minister on 'a significant moment in our national story'. The first MP to put a question to Sunak at Prime Minister's Questions was Alan Whitehead, the veteran Labour MP for the constituency of Southampton Test. Whitehead noted that many of his constituents would take pride in his 'being the first Prime Minister of South Asian heritage' as well as a Southampton FC supporter. The new Prime Minister's response picked up only the mention of his footballing allegiance, noting that the new Leader of the House, Penny Mordaunt, supported their rivals Portsmouth. When Sunak did briefly comment directly on the historic nature of his achievement, a week after taking office, he placed some emphasis on the value of this British social norm of trying not to notice it too much. Sunak said he found it 'wonderful' that his first formal engagement as Prime Minister was to be pictured attending the Diwali reception that had been organised by his predecessor. 'As chancellor I was able to light my Diwali Diyas [lamps] on the steps of Downing Street. It said something wonderful about our country that that was possible, but also that it wasn't a big deal. It was in a sense gosh, this is great, but also that's just Britain. Hopefully it is a source of collective pride across the country,' he told *The Times* in his first interview as Prime Minister.

The irrelevance of faith?

Rishi Sunak is the fifty-seventh Prime Minister of the United Kingdom in the three centuries since Robert Walpole effectively invented the role by so dominating politics in the early eighteenth century. Sunak is the first of Walpole's successors to practise a non-Christian faith in office. This generated remarkably little public comment.

Sunak is the second ethnic minority Prime Minister after Benjamin Disraeli, a century and a half ago. Disraeli identified with his Jewish background and certainly faced some anti-Semitic prejudice in politics, though his baptism into the Anglican Church as a Christian, aged 13, reflected the perceived practical necessity of religious assimilation in the nineteenth century for those of Jewish heritage who wanted to enter the legal profession or public life.

The absence of any objection to a Prime Minister of a minority faith from any public voice with any profile or status is a significant long-term shift. Despite the precedent of Disraeli a century earlier, Nigel Lawson had felt his ethnic heritage was a barrier to his own leadership prospects as a tax-cutting Chancellor in the late 1980s. 'I thought of the job but believed the party at that time wouldn't want someone of Jewish descent as leader,' he was to tell Margaret Thatcher's biographer Charles Moore in

retirement.[4] That Thatcher was the MP for Finchley had reinforced her own philo-Semitism, but Harold Macmillan's gripe
that Thatcher's Cabinet 'contained more Old Estonians than Old
Etonians' encapsulated a cultural tolerance of casual anti-Semitism among his generation of Tory grandees into the 1980s.

Even a decade and a half ago, Tony Blair waited until after he
left Downing Street to become a Roman Catholic. An earlier
conversion would have raised some constitutional issues, even
though Sunak's Hinduism does not. Reforms introduced in 2007
mean that Prime Ministers no longer choose between two names
for ecclesiastical appointments, but simply rubber-stamp the
choice of the Crown Nominations Committee. But a Catholic
Prime Minister would still have to recuse themselves from that
purely symbolic role. The Roman Catholic Relief Act of 1829
continues to bar any person professing the Catholic faith from
advising the monarch directly or indirectly on Church appointments, though this outdated hangover on the statute books of
Britain's long history of anti-Catholic discrimination is not
accompanied by any parallel prohibition on a Prime Minister
who is Hindu or Muslim, Sikh or Jewish, or indeed a professed
atheist.

That Britain now has a Hindu Prime Minister was a much
bigger theme in the Indian press than here in Britain. The lack of
British discussion of this had several causes. Sunak's public profile
had been very much as the Chancellor who had to deal with the
Covid pandemic, including the furlough scheme. Hinduism is a
somewhat esoteric faith to many in Britain, with British Hindus
and Sikhs often being the subject of positive 'good minority'
stereotyping. It seems likely that a Prime Minister who was
Muslim would have seen more discussion of their faith background, though the low-key response to Sunak becoming
premier may benefit those from Muslim backgrounds too. Keir
Starmer's openness about his lack of religious faith has generated

almost no public comment either. The lack of interest in this significant historical 'first' was largely a reflection of increasing secularism in British public life; it also reflected some uncertainty and awkwardness about the boundaries of legitimate discussion of faith in politics and the media even though our age of personality politics discusses every other aspect of a leader's background and character with little inhibition. Indeed, a much more heated argument about faith, rights and policy dominated the opening of the SNP leadership contest to choose a Scottish First Minister, with the surprising twist that scrutiny of the Scottish Presbyterian candidate Kate Forbes's socially conservative views boosted the prospects of the Scottish Asian Muslim contender Humza Yousaf.

Considerably more attention has been paid to Sunak's education and wealth than to his faith. Sunak's is a story of upward social mobility though it lacks some of the romance of the 'son of a bus driver' journeys of his former Cabinet colleague Sajid Javid or the Mayor of London Sadiq Khan, since it is a journey from the middle classes to the stratosphere of the global elite. It began in the professional British Indian middle classes as the son of a GP and a pharmacist, before his schooling at the elite Winchester College private school helped to provide a platform for educational success at Oxford and Stanford, followed by personal wealth via hedge funds, before a love marriage connected him to India's billionaire classes. Sunak is the richest Prime Minister in modern political history. He was the first serving Prime Minister to appear on the *Sunday Times* Rich List, a joint entry with his wife, with an estimated joint wealth of £730 million.[5] One would have to go back to at least the Earl of Rosebery, in 1895, who had married a Rothschild, to find a potential competitor.

Was Britain ready?

Yet whether Britain was ready for an Asian Prime Minister was in question, until it happened.

The 'no big deal' response reflected a widely held social norm. When British Future had asked people about views of a hypothetical ethnic minority prime minister, a quarter of people said this would be a positive symbol of social progress while a surly one in ten saw it as negative. The majority view, of six out of ten respondents, was that ethnicity should be considered irrelevant. Ethnic minority respondents were evenly divided between seeing this as a positive symbol of social progress (43 per cent), or irrelevant to the merits of who should get the job (39 per cent), having been asked to choose between interpretations that could overlap for many people.

One question was whether this claim to non-discrimination really extended to those who would make the choice in the Conservative Party. 'Do you think the members of your party are ready to select a brown man, Rishi?' the barrister Jolyon Maugham had tweeted as the recently resigned Chancellor launched his leadership campaign. In response to criticism, Maugham deleted the message, saying that his intended point was that 'we should all want to encourage greater representation of people of colour leading all political parties'. Maugham accepted that his message to Sunak had not felt especially encouraging, though he wished to hold Sunak's party to account over racism and prejudice, and continued to doubt that party members would judge minority candidates on their merits.

It was argued that the manner of Sunak's accession left those questions unresolved. After all, he lost the leadership election to Liz Truss, by 57 per cent to 43 per cent, after having been the frontrunner among members of parliament. The idea that race played any significantly decisive role in Truss's defeat of Sunak falls apart if properly scrutinised. Truss beat Sunak primarily by telling members more of what they wanted to hear, and Sunak's 43 per cent personal vote was clearly the floor rather than the ceiling for an Asian candidate. (Nobody would suggest that Liz Truss's 57 per cent of the vote included every member who would consider voting for any female leadership candidate, after all.)

The year 2022 had proved a roller-coaster one for Sunak's standing with party members, even though his ethnicity remained constant throughout. Ironically, it was his links to California and his US Green Card, more than his Indian heritage, that saw Sunak at risk of being characterised as what Theresa May had once pejoratively called a 'citizen of nowhere'. Sunak had enjoyed almost universal acclaim as the Covid Chancellor – his net approval rating with party members peaked at a record and almost unanimous 95 per cent – but his role in bringing down Boris Johnson sharply polarised opinion. That party members preferred outsider candidate Kemi Badenoch, a black British woman, to either Truss or Sunak by the end of the contest appears to be clear proof that political ideology was driving more votes than candidate ethnicity. A month after the leadership contest, polls showed that a majority of party members now preferred Sunak to Truss, after the mini-budget went wrong, which offers further proof that a majority were not disqualifying him on grounds of race. Yet commentators who felt Sunak had clearly been a stronger candidate all along still subjectively felt that race was probably the key factor in his defeat. It is partly because different people prioritise different things in political leadership that we can often find their political preferences incomprehensible. That the Conservative Party chose Iain Duncan Smith over Ken Clarke, or indeed Boris Johnson over Jeremy Hunt, tended to baffle those outside of the party too.

Having an Asian Prime Minister does not make Britain a post-racial nirvana. Research for the Nuffield Election Studies shows that ethnic minority candidates can suffer an electoral 'ethnic penalty' from public prejudice. It reports a deficit of 3.6 per cent – a loss of around 1 in 33 votes – for first-time ethnic minority Conservative local constituency candidates in the 2017 General Election.[6] The Conservatives have shown a preference for fielding minority candidates in safe seats with large majorities: an effective strategy to increase parliamentary diversity that neutralises penalty effects at the margin. The same academic study found no net penalty for Labour candidates in 2017. That difference reflects both the more liberal views on race of left-leaning voters, reinforced by a higher ethnic minority vote share. Studies over time show that the ethnic penalty diminishes or disappears once incumbent MPs seek re-election, because familiarity and contact can mitigate casual prejudices faced by first-time candidates. National political figures benefit from that dynamic too. Sunak's initial polls as Prime Minister showed that he was more popular than his party by a wide margin.

So ethnic prejudice can play a significant marginal role, but those with the most progressive political views intuitively feel that the scale of public and electoral prejudice is probably much wider. The More in Common network found that 81 per cent of voters say they would vote for a party led by a hypothetical ethnic minority leader while 8 per cent doubted they would. There was less confidence that other people were as fair-minded: 54 per cent thought most other voters would do so too, while a third felt the average voter would not. The sixth of the population characterised by More in Common as 'progressive activist' were the most likely both to be fine with an ethnic minority Prime Minister themselves – 95 per cent to 5 per cent – and to be least confident in the average citizen. Forty-eight per cent of progressive activists felt that most people might vote for a minority leader, while 44 per cent felt that the median voter probably wouldn't do so.

Vigilance about the persistence of prejudice or racism is valuable, but alarmism is not. Excessive progressive pessimism on this scale has directly regressive consequences for ethnic minorities in public life. This type of 'imputed prejudice' – the exaggerated perception of the scale of public prejudice – is much underestimated as being among the key brakes on ethnic minority progress in politics in the quarter of a century after 1987 until progress accelerated after 2010. For it was not just direct discrimination that held black and Asian candidates back. Nice people in party selectorates worrying about whether the voters were ready for a black or Asian candidate was often as significant.

This progressive pessimism is also likely to contribute to the mysterious phenomenon of the glass ceiling effect on the left. David Cameron's successful effort to increase diversity in the Conservative Party was motivated by wanting to catch up with Labour's stronger record on representation. Still today, half of Labour MPs are women, compared to a quarter of Conservatives. One in five Labour MPs are black, Asian or mixed race, compared to around one in fifteen Conservatives (6 per cent). Despite Labour's stronger overall record on gender and ethnic diversity, it has persistently been the Conservatives who have seen ethnic minorities break through to the very top first. That the Conservatives had the first female and ethnic minority Prime Minister may be a coincidence, but this is starting to look like a pattern. Labour led the way in changing the image of what an MP looked like, with the first post-war ethnic minority MPs and, especially, the large intake of women in 1997, but parties of the left may still have a narrower, more cautious and safer archetype of what leadership, competence and electability look like. One regressive consequence of excessive progressive pessimism concerning public norms in relation to overt discrimination is that

progressive parties seem more likely to see ethnic minority leadership as a 'risk' until their conservative rivals have proved it is safe.

Beyond competing grievances

Rishi Sunak's rise, and the way we talk about what more ethnic
minority faces in high places does and does not mean, illumi-
nates several issues about diversity, representation and
opportunity in Britain. The lack of drama around Sunak's
premiership reinforces the idea that ethnic diversity, like gender
diversity, has become a new norm at the top table. This is a
significant, rapid and remarkably recent change in British politics. A 'role model' theory – if you can't see it, you can't be it – is
often applied to business, media and culture. On that logic, more
diversity at the apex of political power will influence what future
generations see as 'normal', whatever the politics of those at the
top. Some on the left argue that more diversity in high office can
be actively regressive if ethnic minority ministers feel a particular
pressure to outflank their colleagues on the right. This line of
argument easily slips into patronising or pathologising ethnic
minority politicians who hold different political views. If ethnic
diversity is a new normal, there will be black and Asian left-wing,
centrist and right-wing voices across the factions of the major
parties. There are plenty of strong critiques of the immigration
policies of Theresa May, Priti Patel or Suella Braverman that do
not depend on holding ethnic minority politicians to different
standards to their colleagues, just as one could reasonably expect
right-of-centre critics of Sadiq Khan or David Lammy to challenge them as they might Keir Starmer or Emily Thornberry
rather than on different grounds. It seems to me a useful general
rule to not make criticisms of political opponents on the basis of
their ethnicity or faith rather than their politics and policies.

Britain has become more open at the top, certainly by gender and ethnic diversity, in the last decade than it was before the 1990s. Its political and professional elites have opened up for those who share the educational credentials and professional networks of the existing in-group, whatever their ethnic or faith background or gender. That is one kind of advance for opportunity in public life. What is much more challenging is how to extend fair chances and more equal opportunities across educational and social class divides. Must we choose between these priorities for progress? Ironically, one of the barriers has become how often social class (and sometimes the position of the white working class in particular) is deployed as a counter-argument if disparities for ethnic minorities and women are being highlighted, but it is too often quickly dropped once race is not the topic. This creates an arid zero-sum politics of competing grievances, where minority or majority disadvantages are set up as causes we must choose between.

The principle we need is one of fair chances for all and the removal of unfair barriers across all dimensions of opportunity and disadvantage, and the practical means to pursue that in practice. Social class remains a talking point, rather than an actionable priority. This is partly because how we talk about class tends to mix up many different objective and subjective factors about identity, income and social status, including what job we do, our family background, or where we grew up and went to school. As a result, we often lack consistent, comparable data to track opportunity and inequalities by geography, educational background and socio-economic status. Changing that is an essential foundation to strategies for fair chances that try to tackle the barriers across different under-represented groups. The Social Mobility Commission, for example, recommends using parental occupation when aged around 14 as the most illuminating simple measure of socio-economic background.

Change needs to be substantive as well as symbolic, but that argument will be less persuasive if made from spheres of economic or cultural power that are not keeping up with the pace set by national politics on diversity at the top – such as the media, academia and civic society. Elected, representative politics is much more ethnically diverse than the backroom special advisers or the journalists who cover it. Word-of-mouth networks tend to self-recruit in their own image. Open recruitment and competition can break that down. Progress in one sphere should catalyse pressure to emulate it. Less than five years ago, the majority of FTSE 100 boardrooms were all white. A shared commitment to change this has helped to tackle the 'affinity bias' whereby boards recruited from their own networks and in their own image. More needs to happen to embed that progress. Yet no FTSE 100 company based in the UK has yet had a British-born ethnic minority chief executive. The contrast with a succession of ethnic minority Chancellors is striking. Major charities, for example, lag behind the public and private sector on almost every available indicator of ethnic minority leadership, with no comparable sector-wide commitments even to eliminate all-white boards. There is certainly no shortage of anxious talk about diversity deficits. The comfort zone response has often been to acknowledge wider social and structural causes affecting society. That has not turned into rigorous analysis of the specific reasons why charities lag behind nor has it been a sufficient priority to trigger effective action to monitor and narrow these gaps.

We should make the case too that social inequality is corrosive of patriotism whenever inequalities are so stark and persistent that they cannot credibly be justified in terms of effort, contribution and fairness. That may sound like an idea of the left – but it ought to be an insight able to reach across much of the mainstream political spectrum. After all, it is Disraeli's famous description of the 'two nations' in his 1840s novel *Sybil* that exemplifies most concisely how and why this is the case. He wrote:

> Two nations; between whom there is no intercourse and no sympathy; who are as ignorant of each other's habits, thoughts, and feelings, as if they were dwellers in different zones, or inhabitants of different planets; who are formed by a different breeding, are fed by a different food, are ordered by different manners, and are not governed by the same laws.[7]

Disraeli's description of the social gulf between the rich and the poor is one of the first descriptions of what the political scientists in this century have come to call 'affective polarisation'. It may be useful to recognise how these 'them and us' dynamics can underpin the types of socio-economic segregation and cultural polarisation that make it decreasingly possible to believe that we are a community of fate where our lives are sufficiently intertwined where what happens to you matters to me. So, patriots should care about inequality across all of its dimensions. Those who want to narrow the social class divides in our society might find it useful to reflect on the value of institutions and identities that can foster and underpin a sense of a common life and mutual obligations.

Rishi Sunak will be conscious both that he has had wider opportunities than were possible for previous generations and that few people in Britain today have the opportunities that he has. If we want an inclusive politics of fairness, we must do more to challenge the idea of choosing between which groups we want to break down the barriers to equal opportunities for.

10

Disunited Kingdom

What would being British mean without the Union?

If I ever want to feel more English, heading to Scotland can be
one of the best ways to achieve that these days. Britain is a strange
kind of country, where almost everyone has two flags and two
national identities. Even Orwell, who wrote as often about
English and British identity as any other major twentieth-century writer, could breezily assert in *The Lion and the Unicorn* that
national differences were essentially small local matters of an
essentially regional character.

> ... even Welsh and Scottish readers are likely to have been
> offended because I have used the word 'England' oftener than
> 'Britain', as though the whole population dwelt in London and
> the Home Counties and neither north nor west possessed a
> culture of its own ... But somehow these differences fade away
> the moment that any two Britons are confronted by a European.
> It is very rare to meet a foreigner, other than an American, who
> can distinguish between English and Scots or even English and
> Irish. Looked at from the outside, even the cockney and the
> Yorkshireman have a strong family resemblance.

Few writers would try to assert that today. Orwell's biographer Bernard Crick, not least as an Englishman in Edinburgh in the pre-devolution period, was among the most influential voices to foresee how the multi-national nature of the United Kingdom would once again become a central rather than peripheral theme of British politics.[1] Crick argued that the United Kingdom had been not just a multi-national state for three hundred years but consequently a multicultural one for two centuries too[2] – and there may still be lessons from that long past for the challenges we face now.

Lost in translation? The different Britishness

Talking about being British can get lost in translation across the nations of the UK. Are we even talking about the same thing any more? This is not an entirely new phenomenon. For some decades now, the two groups tending to report a somewhat stronger sense of British identity than anybody else has been the Protestants of Northern Ireland, and ethnic minorities from Commonwealth backgrounds in England's cities. Yet the murals and painted red, white and blue kerbstones of Ulster's Loyalists, and Birmingham's pride in the invention of the British Balti, represent different ideas and associations about what makes us British.

The distinctions between varieties of Britishness have become more marked still in the last decade. In 2016, feeling more British meant you were more likely to vote Remain in England, or more likely to vote Leave in Scotland. Having a stronger British identity has precisely the inverse sociology in Scotland – being older, more Christian, white, more traditional and more Eurosceptic – and England, where it denotes a younger, left-leaning identity, stronger in university cities and among Hindus, Sikhs and Muslims. Scottishness unites in Scotland, while British

identity divides people along political lines. The pattern is different in England, where British identity is broadly but lightly held,
and the intensity of English identity is a stronger predictor of
political choices, while the relationship of the Welsh language,
identity and politics in Wales has shifted somewhat in the wake
of Brexit too.

Yet perhaps one benefit of an increasingly disunited United
Kingdom is to have made the rules of being British and stating
what that means much clearer. This is now, explicitly, a Union of
consent. So we will remain British, *as long as* that is what majorities in each of the constituent nations want. To put it another
way, we will remain British, *only if* that is what majorities in each
of the constituent nations want. The United Kingdom has no
selfish strategic interest in Northern Ireland, and has pledged to
facilitate the reunification of Ireland should that be the mutual
will of north and south. The only barrier to Scotland or Northern
Ireland – or Wales, or indeed England – leaving the UK is the
clear and settled will of the nation to do so. A liberal patriotism
can regard this as a positive feature of the UK, compared to the
stand-off in Spain over Catalonia, where there is no such foundational agreement on how either identity or constitutional
arguments can be settled.

Britain is now a much more consciously complex and
multi-national polity than it was even a quarter of a century ago.
What this means is that whether the United Kingdom has a
future as well as a past involves a clash of patriotisms. That
contest might take different forms. It could become a heart and
head clash – between identity and economics and interests. Or it
might be a question of whether British patriotisms can be
combined and inter-dependent, or whether independence is
necessary for any patriotism to be authentic and fully realised. *To
every nation a state?* On that principle, any multi-national state is
an inherently unstable thing, though its break-up might be as

conciliatory as the velvet divorce of the Czechs and Slovaks or as bloody as the collapse of Yugoslavia, or anything in between. So the future of the United Kingdom might depend on deciding whether anybody could ever really make a multi-national patriotism work – and secure mutual consent for what that should mean in practice.

Union lost: lessons from Ireland's troubled history

'Irish history is something no Englishman should forget and no Irishman should remember.' I tried to take George Bernard Shaw's advice, though it was tricky to work out the exact balance of remembering and forgetting his idiom would prescribe to my teenage English, Irish Catholic, half-Indian self. But I did find myself immersively captivated by Irish history, literature and culture. I felt connected to the worlds of Wilde and Shaw, Synge and Heaney, though the mystical turn of Yeats largely escaped me. My Irish hero became Charles Stuart Parnell, the Home Ruler, who Gladstone had freed from Kilmainham Jail in order to advocate for Home Rule but whose career fell to divorce, scandal and an early death.

There was never really a serious effort to secure Irish consent for the Union with Ireland. The implicit promise to treat Ireland equally within the Union was frustrated immediately by delaying the implicit promise of Catholic emancipation for three decades. The Irish felt it was very clear that the 1840s famine would have been treated differently had the humanitarian emergency fallen on Lancashire. Once the franchise was extended in the 1860s, there was a clear settled Irish will for Home Rule, put consistently at the ballot box, for four decades.

Gladstone spent fully two and a half hours in 1886 on a great appeal to a divided Commons to recognise that. 'Tightening the tie is frequently the means of making it burst, while relaxing the tie is very frequently the way to provide for its durability,' he said, arguing that the Home Rulers are the Unionists. 'We conscientiously believe that there are Unionists and Disunionists; but that it is our policy that leads to union and yours to separation.'[3] If Gladstone was heeding Edmund Burke's famous warning over America – 'not whether you have a right to render your people miserable, but whether it is not your interest to make them happy' – Burke's own Tory descendants could never recognise that argument in the case of Ireland. So Gladstone could never prevail while a fully hereditary Lords held an absolute veto, and recognised no democratic conventions against its use. Even once Home Rule did pass the Commons in 1893, the Lords rejected it on second reading by 419 votes to 41.

Once the Parliament Act of 1911 meant that Home Rule could pass, all hell broke out. 'There are things stronger than Parliamentary majorities,' thundered Bonar Law, the leader of His Majesty's opposition, whose commitment to controlling the destiny of the Empire extended to inciting Ulster's loyalists to take up arms against an Act carrying the royal seal, with the King's consent for what was in essence a treasonous plot, ultimately impeded only by the Great War. Still, Parnell's successor Redmond urged the Irish to the trenches to earn Ireland's freedom by fighting for King and Country. After Easter 1916 the Home Rulers were swept away by a Sinn Fein landslide.

Had Home Rule been passed, constitutionally, it would probably have provided a less bloody means of divorce, rather than an enduring federation of the isles. 'No man has the right to fix a boundary to the march of a nation' are the famous words featured on Parnell's statue on Dublin's O'Connell Street. Ireland could have followed a Canadian path towards independence, without the martyrs and blood sacrifices created by General Maxwell overseeing summary executions in Dublin Castle in 1916. The hard historical truth is that both polities on the island of Ireland owed their existence, in significant part, to the threat or the use of arms, however much the heirs of Gladstone and Parnell might regret the many missed opportunities to avoid that.

As a young country, Ireland knew that history mattered. 'In a country that has come of age, history need no longer be a matter of guarding sacred mysteries,' as leading revisionist Roy Foster wrote in 1986. Irish revisionist historians challenged the use of history for incendiary purposes after the Troubles broke out in the north, and they did it with good history too. It was a challenge that modern Ireland needed. A new Ireland emerged in the 1990s, with the opening up to Europe offering more psychological space to escape England's shadow and the pace of the Church's moral collapse.

Northern Ireland remains, for most people in Britain, a far-away country of which we know little, even though it is part of our own state. It would be hard to overstate the level of public ignorance or indifference. Contrary to the media narrative of staunch resistance to the Provos, British public preferences throughout the Troubles were in favour of a united Ireland, as the British Social Attitudes data shows, perhaps largely on the ignoble isolationist grounds of it being more hassle than it was worth.

My Catholic background would have given me a green-tinged view of Ulster. But I became sceptical of my staunchly Catholic mother's view, that the 'six counties' were an illegitimate statelet essentially, because God had drawn the boundaries of the island of Ireland. John Hume became another of my political heroes, showing how passion against injustice could be combined with a commitment to peace, democracy and reconciliation. His reworking of a united Ireland into an agreed Ireland seemed compelling to me. I became more fiercely hostile to the IRA campaign after the IRA's bombing in Warrington in 1993 felt so close to home. Alongside three-year-old Jonathan Ball, the other child murdered, Tim Parry, was a twelve-year-old Evertonian. That bombing had come, cruelly, at a moment when peace had felt tantalisingly close.

Despite that nadir, the 30 years to 2016 were the most positive period in Anglo-Irish and British–Irish relationships in centuries – socially, culturally and politically. The peace settlement in Northern Ireland was an enormous, shared achievement of British and Irish statecraft from 1986 onwards. Even with the most constructive London–Dublin partnership in generations, those outside Northern Ireland could not, ultimately, deliver peace from outside without the will inside Northern Ireland too. The late David Trimble, the first leader of Ulster Unionism in a century to be able to say yes as well as no, and then to make it stick, best described it in his Nobel lecture on being awarded the Nobel Peace Prize, jointly with John Hume, in 1998:

> Both communities must leave it behind, because both created it. Each thought it had good reason to fear the other. As Namier says, the irrational is not necessarily unreasonable. Ulster Unionists, fearful of being isolated on the island, built a solid house, but it was a cold house for Catholics. And northern nationalists, although they had a roof over their heads, seemed to us as if they meant to burn the house down.[4]

The normality of life in Northern Ireland is the most striking thing to outsiders who come to know it a little better. Deepening this has been the great prize of Northern Ireland's imperfect peace. It seems slightly depressing to note that the rest of the UK might have more to learn from Northern Ireland in these increasingly polarised times. That is not to disparage the impressive, if incomplete, strides made in Northern Ireland to reduce the social distance between two mutually suspicious and excessively segregated communities, but it may reflect some regression in identity clashes elsewhere. In recent years, efforts across the Republic of Ireland and Northern Ireland to mark 'the decade of centenaries' – the coincidence of the Easter Rising and the Somme, the birth of the Republic and Northern Ireland, partition and civil war – offer perhaps the best model to date for engaging with contentious and controversial history, without avoidance, in a way that is educative, respectful of deeply held identities, while both recognising and defusing the potential for unconstructive conflict.

Northern Ireland has an imperfect peace, perhaps a fragile one. I found it disheartening that a recent poll revealed that seven out of ten Catholics felt there had been no alternative to the armed struggle of the IRA, though the under-45s, who have come to adulthood after it ended, were much more likely to think this than those who had an adult memory of the Troubles. Brexit has deeply polarised politics across communities once again. Even when institutions work, enforced power-sharing (reducing the power of voters to vote a government in or out) is a pragmatic acknowledgement of the fragility of trust between communities, perhaps freezing the politics of Northern Ireland while the society evolves. The 'neithers', the third identity, have a growing appeal across generations but a more muted voice in politics than in business, law and civic society.

Whether Northern Ireland will still be within the UK, or in a new Irish Republic, a quarter- or half-century from now is unknown. Serious discussion of the form that a united Ireland might take in practice is only slowly beginning to emerge. The achievement of the last quarter-century of a fragile peace, after a quarter of a century of violence, has been to use devolution and cross-community governance to blur the boundaries of what had seemed a binary existential choice. There are some grounds for optimism that there is a broader understanding that John Hume's vision of 'an agreed Ireland' must ultimately prevail, whether

Northern Ireland's future is within the United Kingdom or outside of it.

Scotland's stalemate

Scotland had a much happier, much luckier experience of the Union than Ireland[5] – or indeed than Wales too. Few could doubt that Scotland was still culturally Scotland within the Union.[6] Any idea of consciously rebranding Scots as 'North Britons' quickly fizzled out. Scots were among the most enthusiastic pioneers, partners and beneficiaries of the Empire project, while it lasted. The polemical claim that the Scottish nation was 'bought and sold by English gold' might appeal on Burns Night itself. So there can be little doubt of the broad, everyday Scottish public consent for the United Kingdom for most of the twentieth century, nor that there were important fractures in the consent for how Scotland was governed by the 1980s. The nadir of modern Scottish identity came in 1978 and 1979, when the farcical hubris of Ally McLeod's promise to win the World Cup in Argentina combined with the failure of the 1979 devolution referendum (a 52 per cent to 48 per cent vote in favour did not meet a new turnout threshold, which stipulated that the vote in favour had to be 40 per cent of the eligible electorate). The experience of Thatcherism sparked a mobilisation across civic Scotland across the 1980s and 1990s in the Scottish Constitutional Convention, which was able to deliver a clear proof that devolution had become the broad and settled will of Scotland once a new government could put the question – with 74 per cent voting for devolution, and almost two-thirds for the new parliament to have tax-raising powers.

The Scottish National Party did not take part in the Scottish Constitutional Convention, but became converts to devolution, taking the chance to govern Scotland a decade later. The SNP deserves credit for how its 1990s reshaping and modernisation of the Scottish independence project significantly contributed to making Scotland's dominant expressions of political and cultural nationalism decisively civic rather than ethnic. The SNP had been a Eurosceptic party that objected to Scotland being taken into the EEC by London without Scottish consent in 1973. A generation later it had become a pro-European party that opposed Brexit on similar grounds. But by the 1990s, the idea of Scotland in Europe made a modern independence project more plausible, at least while the UK was a member of the EU. Scotland is much less ethnically diverse than England, with about 5 per cent of the population from visible minorities, yet there was a concerted effort to recognise Asians as new Scots, and celebrate those who chose to don Tartan.

After a knife-edge defeat for Québécois independence – by just 54,000 votes out of nearly 5 million (50.6 per cent to 49.4 per cent) in 1995, veteran leader Jacques Parizeau lamented a defeat he attributed to 'money and the ethnic vote', before resigning in the furore over his lapse into ethnic nationalism. Scotland's 2014 vote – 55 per cent to 45 per cent – was not so close. This civic emphasis was confirmed when the Scotland Referendum Study showed that a slim majority (52 per cent) of the Scottish-born had voted for independence. The SNP fielded MSP Christian Allard, born in France, to argue that this was of no consequence. 'Scotland is the country of everyone who lives here, regardless of where they were born, and we take decisions on our future together.'[7] A more contentious question was how far anti-English sentiment had been marginalised in the public articulation of modern Scottish politics. It had been a perspective memorably expressed by the character Renton in Irvine Walsh's *Trainspotting*: 'Ah don't hate the English. They're just wankers. We are colonised by wankers. We can't even pick a decent, vibrant, healthy culture to be colonised by.' SNP leaders worked hard to remove such sentiment from the public case, though opponents claimed that 'Westminster' made the old argument in code.

The 2014 referendum galvanised, mobilised and polarised Scotland. The 84 per cent turnout was impressive. There were very different experiences of the referendum campaign. What felt like an inspiring new mobilisation of a vibrant political movement for many supporters of independence, despite the disappointment of the outcome, felt for others an angry, deeply polarising event in which political division was totalising, affecting family dynamics, friendships and workplaces. The result undoubtedly demonstrated the fragility of consent for the UK. It was a much more transactional than emotional decision to stay. The No campaign made almost no identity argument at all, because it mattered little to swing voters. I was also struck by just how late anybody in 2014 noticed the referendum, which was mostly below the radar until there were three weeks to go. I attended the one pro-UK rally in Trafalgar Square, a genial occasion, addressed by Dan Snow and Sir Bob Geldof. A few thousand people present were pleased to have found some way to recognise that such an important referendum was taking place. But I doubt many people there were under any illusion that this expression of solidarity might decisively influence swing voters in Dundee or Fife.

Scotland's binary stand-off

Scotland has been stuck in an exhausting, binary stalemate. That there were national election or referendum campaigns in Scotland in 2014, 2015, 2016 (twice), 2017, 2019 and 2021 risks voter fatigue. The consolation prize for the losing 45 per cent was an SNP landslide in Scotland's Westminster elections and the continued governance of Scotland, but with no decisive shift resulting from Brexit or the Covid pandemic on the question of independence itself. Whether or when Scotland might vote again on independence in the years to come is unknown. Ultimately, the political and legal skirmishes over the process and the timing of a future referendum are a second-order question. If a sustained majority of Scots want a referendum, so as to vote for independence, that will happen.

Another Scottish referendum would contain many echoes of the Brexit referendum. The irony is that most of those involved would be using the opposite soundbites and arguments. The fear in a pro-Brexit Downing Street is that they know how to defeat the sort of campaign that they may have to support. Scotland's SNP government have been fierce critics of the chaos of departing a union without sufficient preparation, but creating a new state and renegotiating its relationships across Britain after the UK clearly presents much deeper challenges than leaving the European Union did.

So these parallel arguments are not identical. The Remain campaign could not land their argument concerning the economic costs of leaving, due to future trade barriers, partly because the UK was a net contributor to the EU budget. That the United Kingdom is worth a net transfer of £4,330 per person per year – on the Scottish government's official Government Expenditure and Revenue Scotland (GERS) figures – makes the economic cost of departure more tangible.

A future Scottish referendum would be largely decided by the votes of almost half of the population (44 per cent) who feel 'more Scottish than British', amid fierce arguments about democracy and identity, as well as currency and pensions. Ultimately, the UK's choice for Brexit has made independence emotionally more attractive yet practically much more difficult than when 'independence in Europe' offered an overarching framework for some of the foundational future relationships within the UK too before 2016. The questions of currency, pensions, trade and borders would all be more challenging in 2024 than 2014. The idea of 'independence within Europe' may give way again to an exploration of devo-max options for quasi-independence within Britain.

The case for another independence referendum has starkly polarised nationalists and unionist opinion in the years since 2014, but some influencers within the independence movement are now exploring alternative paths to the push for a further binary referendum if a future Westminster government proposes a new constitutional process. 'There's a difference between winning a campaign and building a nation,' Stephen Noon, architect of the 2014 Yes campaign has said. 'You don't build a nation by creating two 50/50 sides. If we go down a process which is about loggerheads, and we scrape a victory in a referendum, and we then find the relationship with England is difficult, post-Brexit vote style, I don't think that's the best start to an independent country.'[8] The logic of that argument is to hold another referendum if and when there is evidence for a sustained majority for independence in Scotland, so that the vote becomes an exercise in testing and ratifying it, rather than being a vehicle for an underdog campaign to try to secure a majority. This had briefly been Nicola Sturgeon's instinct in the wake of the 2014 vote: that it would take 60 per cent support to reopen the question. Sturgeon's departure as First Minister this spring may see an increasing acknowledgement among SNP leaders that the viable legal route to independence depends on broadening sustained support, rather than challenging the UK government's scepticism that the case for a referendum has been made. Civic voices who are neutral on independence, and some of those opposed to it, could make a constructive contribution to seeking to build a new 'rules of the game' consensus on benchmarks or processes for agreeing how to evidence a settled consensus for a new referendum.

There are voices that would campaign for the UK who believe the question should be a less existential one too. 'For the people who favour independence, the constitution trumps everything, but for those of us who want to keep the UK together, it's not, for most of us, what defines our politics. I'm much more interested in whether we're ending poverty than what flag that support for families arrives under', Kirsty McNeill, chair of the advisory board of Our Scottish Future, told me.

Should the question be put to the public again, supporters and opponents of Scottish independence will naturally focus on how to persuade 50.1 per cent of Scots to vote their way in any future referendum. Civic Scotland will want to invest some energy in how a society keeps living and working together as it debates the types of existential democratic choices that can split the political nation down the middle.

The United Kingdom has created space for a stronger Scottish political voice and much more Scottish cultural confidence since the 1990s. But it may yet be that voices for de-escalation across the referendum divide can make the case that an effort to secure overlapping consent within Scotland and across the UK for an evolving constitutional settlement could provide a more constructive focus over the next five years than another referendum.

Wales: lessons in involving the losers

I have always felt mildly jealous about not being Welsh, though I could probably be said to have access to more than enough national identities to be getting along with. I can attribute this mostly to Mr Flavin, a great PE teacher, rugby coach and enormously enthusiastic propagandist for the golden age of Welsh rugby, J. P. R. Williams and all that. It was proximity too – growing up in Cheshire, with Rhyl up the coast, not just having beaches, but what in that era seemed a rather magical wave machine in the leisure centre – that influenced me. I saw in person Wales play international football at Wrexham, with their cross-section of Everton, Liverpool and Manchester United stars, a decade before I watched England play at Wembley. My empathy for Wales was later reinforced by ending up studying at Jesus College, Oxford, without knowing it had been founded as Oxford's 'Welsh college' back in 1571. This continued to be reflected in its reputation for Celtic studies and commitment to Welsh access schemes, as well as by it's being a hub for most Welsh people for miles around for Six Nations games. Of course, my imaginary Welshness rarely extended beyond marking St David's Day and by my joining in with supporting Wales in the rugby. The Welsh do have by far the best anthem, and it is much easier to learn the words than John Redwood ever realised. I have maintained my secret support for Wales at rugby, even against England, somehow imagining that I am finally getting one over on Norman Tebbit and his cricket test.

The 1979 referendum in Wales rejected devolution by an enormously wide margin of four to one, with Neil Kinnock the most prominent opponent of devolution. Widespread lack of confidence in Wales's political leaders – a sense among many across Wales that Cardiff's elites might be more distant and less trusted even than those in Westminster – remained a significant factor in 1997. While three-quarters of Scotland voted for devolution, Wales's assent was on a knife-edge, being carried by less than 7,000 votes out of 1.2 million cast, 50.3 per cent to 49.7 per cent on only a 50 per cent turnout. It was recognised that a National Assembly of Wales would be on very shaky ground with

such narrow support. What happened after 1997 in Wales represents a sustained and remarkably successful effort to secure 'loser's
consent' after a knife-edge result. As Richard Wyn Jones has written, 'the enlightened efforts of Welsh home rulers to build
legitimacy has helped establish devolution – after the fact – as the
"settled will" of the country's electorate'.⁹ The fragility of the new
assembly was clear to Ron Davies and Peter Hain in the Welsh
office, so significant efforts were made to proceed on a cross-
party basis. There was already significantly broader public
support for the Assembly once it opened in 1999. Wanting devolution abolished, which had commanded the support of half of
those voting in 1997, shrank to around one in six. By 2011,
almost two-thirds voted for the Welsh parliament to exercise
fuller powers, albeit on an anaemic turnout of 35 per cent.

This broadening of consent for devolution primarily reflected
a desire for the recognition of Wales's national status, much more
than it did public confidence with the weak performance of the
devolved institutions themselves, impeded by a muddled and
inadequate framework of powers and responsibilities. The Brexit
referendum of 2016 – in which Wales joined England with a
vote to Leave, with almost all of the Welsh political, civic and
economic elites on the other side – demonstrated that identity
and socio-economic divides in Wales remain underacknowl-
edged. There has been an increased post-Brexit polarisation
around national identities, both British and Welsh. Independence
is increasingly part of the public conversation, but remains a long
way from viability in practice or from securing the breadth of
engagement it would need across Wales.

Had Wales rejected devolution again in 1997, or failed to
broaden consent for it afterwards, it would surely have been
much harder to secure the increased cultural confidence of Wales
that has been evident in culture and sport outside the political
sphere. The Welsh experience may offer insights into both the

opportunities and difficulties of how a multi-national union proceeds. Welsh leaders have seen the importance of joining up the conversations about the future of the United Kingdom but have struggled to be heard in a UK-wide conversation, largely dominated by the aftermath of Scotland's 2014 referendum. The future of Wales's voice and place within a 'rest of the United Kingdom' polity would become a more acute problem in the event of Scottish independence.

What does England want?

England and English identity have changed and evolved over a thousand years of history, during three hundred years of the UK, during the broadening out over the last half-century of who is English across ethnic and faith lines, and in adapting in the twenty-five years or so since 1999 to the UK becoming a more multi-national state and society. The question of the voice and role of the largest of the British nations remains the hole in the polo mint of our shifting, multi-national United Kingdom. England has been the missing dimension of the asymmetric devolved settlement. Why was so little said about England for so long? For a long time, it was a product of confidence. Once Ireland's departure from the UK meant that England made up 80 per cent of the population of the United Kingdom after 1922, Englishness rarely felt challenged from within, until national questions from the 'Celtic fringe' began to re-emerge from the mid-1970s.

A further period of a muted England arose from a desire to protect the Union. Devolution meant that the English question had to be asked, yet the reluctance to answer it was rooted in a traditional British Unionist instinct to see any rise in national allegiance as setting us on a slippery slope to the break-up of

Britain. A quarter of a century after devolution, it should be clearer that this is a mistaken strategy, which is doing more harm than good to its own cause.

What is often overlooked is that a rise in English identity has made the English British somewhat more like the Welsh and the Scottish. Majorities in Scotland and Wales still value Britishness, but it has become a shared, secondary, multi-national identity, important on civic moments that bring Britain together, such as Remembrance Day. The everyday identity, however, is the national one. There has also been a rebalancing back in England towards a 'both equally' identity. Indeed, census results demonstrate the nuances of English and British identity in England. Seventy-one per cent chose an English-only identity in 2011. In 2021, when the order of the options was reversed, the proportion with a British identity rose to 55 per cent from 19 per cent in 2011, while English-only fell to 15 per cent. Whichever box people tick, in reality both identities are widely held across England.

The English conversation is now happening. But a commonly voiced fear is that the English voice will be angry and atavistic, primarily a form of 'them and us' grievance politics: anti-Europe, anti-Scotland, anti-immigration, anti-Muslim. An asymmetric devolution that treats England as an overdog nation, too big and too ugly to be recognised, will fail to sustain English consent for efforts to negotiate a devolved settlement in Scotland and Wales. A simple sense of fairness suggests that the English also expect to have their say in the decisions we make about our multi-national UK.

So the opportunity to consider an English dimension will be essential if a broader UK-wide settlement is attempted. But the lack of public interest in micro-reforms such as 'English votes for English laws' may reflect that the appetite to see something done for England is first and foremost a question of cultural recognition. Symbols matter when it comes to Englishness. Adopting

'Jerusalem' as an English sporting anthem for English teams, and ceasing to appropriate the British anthem even when playing against Scotland or Wales, should work for everyone. Why not also celebrate St George's Day properly – and make sure that everybody is invited to the party? That could reassure those who fear that expressions of English identity are caricatured as xenophobic, as well as those who worry about whether Englishness can be inclusive.

Support for these simple signals of how England's voice can count would help to open up broader questions about representation and voice. British-wide cultural institutions, from the major political parties, the National Theatre to the BBC, should think about where and when they need a distinctively English dimension, as should the political parties, when making not UK-wide but English policy on issues devolved to Cardiff Bay, Holyrood and Stormont. Politicians might engage substantively with the English question more easily once they realise that they don't need to begin the debate with the constitutional blueprint. Political reform may ultimately be part of the answer too, but to find out what the English want from a reformed UK, we need to create more political and cultural space for English voices to be heard.

Does the UK have a future?

I don't have any great plan or project to 'save the Union'. But I doubt that it is going to be some kind of project that could save it. The future of the United Kingdom will not be a question of putting post-war twentieth-century Britishness, like Humpty Dumpty, back together again. Now that this has become a more complex, multi-national patchwork UK, any successful future British project needs to understand and recognise the appeal of

Scottish, Welsh and English patriotism and governance, and show how and why these add something that is more than the sum of their parts. It will succeed only if that can reach across generations as well as across nations.

There will undoubtedly be more high-profile efforts to get the right powers in the right places, such as the Commission on the Future of the UK led by Gordon Brown, of which I was a member, and various ideas about the forms of citizens' assemblies that can try to make these a project with broader legitimacy and ownership beyond the political classes. Whether these can succeed may make a significant difference to whether a future referendum is held in the next few years, and perhaps to the outcome too. I suspect the core question as to how far such efforts succeed or fail may concern less the nuances and details about how to get the constitutional framework right, and more the emotional choice that underpins them; whether we do or don't think we still have enough in common to make the effort.

There is a rational case for pessimism about the future of the UK in the long run. The generational profile of support for independence and the UK in Scotland has many drivers – surely exacerbated by the identity and cultural conflicts of the Brexit era. Another emerging shift may come from emerging generations for whom devolution was not experienced as a change within the Union but the settled norm from the start of their adult lives. Little attention had been paid to how far the amount of social contact among citizens across the UK nations affects perceptions and attitudes. Different views of the future of the UK by social class, education and socio-economic status may well reflect how much more distant the idea of the United Kingdom is for those least likely to cross its borders for work or education, culture or family.

For the United Kingdom to work, it is probably going to become more of a coalition of identities, values and interests. Yet there is a danger in the future of the United Kingdom turning into a permanent negotiation. It may take a patience that our binary 'winner takes all' political culture rarely values. Endless negotiations can be exhausting if you do not know why you are making the effort.

It will be harder to keep the UK together if conversations about its future only take place in silos in different nations. A British General Election these days is made up of four or five different contests with different party systems across the nations of the UK. If the type of politicians who eagerly pose with flags and tanks to convey their enthusiasm for the Union make arguments that could risk damaging it for the sake of helping to win half a dozen seats in Devon and Cornwall, or the Midlands, then the Union may become still more fragile. The BBC may come under most pressure when trying to do its job, reporting the claims and counter-claims fairly, when the subject is the future of the United Kingdom itself. If the BBC does not attempt to convene a UK-wide, citizen-centred discussion of the future of the United Kingdom that is accessible to the median citizen across the nations – what it would mean in the future if we choose to keep it, and what could happen next if we do not – it is unlikely that anybody else will manage to.

These conversations, and the negotiations we need, are not just across and between the UK nations, but within them too. If an agreed United Kingdom is not possible, then the North of Ireland needs to find its place in an agreed Ireland. If Scotland were one day to vote for independence, by a knife-edge margin such as 51 per cent to 49 per cent, the work of forging an agreed Scotland would have to begin. If trying to develop and rebalance the United Kingdom will take effort and patience, trying to unravel it and negotiate the future relationships on this island will dominate at least a decade of politics and public life. Whatever political choices are made in future, people in England,

Northern Ireland, Scotland and Wales need to find ways to live well together, however we vote in elections and referendums.

Nobody knows what the rest of the UK would feel on the morning after a Yes vote for independence in Scotland. A shrug of the shoulders and a stoic 'keep calm and carry on' spirit? Or might the psychological reverberations, whether liberating or traumatic, run much deeper? Even the simplest symbolic questions have been barely discussed. We would probably not, I guess, take the blue out of the Union Jack (for 'Auld lang syne', perhaps) but what would the 'rest of the United Kingdom', the country formerly known as Great Britain and Northern Ireland, even be called?

There is a rational case for the future of the United Kingdom: that it could continue to operate as a shared umbrella under which different national identities and aspirations can shelter. The strongest arguments for that both/and combination may well remain the practical value of the shelter of the umbrella on rainy days – in the pandemics and financial crises of this century, not just the world wars of the last – as much as its emotional appeal on the high days and holidays that still reflect the shared bonds of a common citizenship, around Remembrance, the monarchy or Team GB in the Olympic Games. There is a practical case too that the business of unravelling it now could be the recipe for a lost decade.

Yet those rational calculations of mutual advantage will not be enough without a sense that the political framework can give due recognition and respect to national identities and aspirations. A multi-national shared citizenship does not need to win a patriotism tug-of-war with our national identities, but we will need to persuade ourselves that we are still at least just 'British enough' to continue to make that effort.

11

A Very British Culture War and How to Call It Off

Would you like to call off the 'culture wars'? Most people would. Few people relish living in a society of ever-increasing conflict about identity, where almost every event becomes one more opportunity to increase the temperature, and to remind each other why people like *us* don't like people like *them*.

But do you *really* want to call off the culture wars? How much? Are you willing to concede or give anything up to achieve that? That might seem a rather unfair question. It probably isn't *you* that needs to change. By far the most popular way to dial down the noise and reduce the heat of the culture wars is for *other people*, who we don't agree with, to stop spouting so much nonsense, so the rest of us can get on with what most people of goodwill can surely agree seems fair and sensible. If your main idea for taking the heat out of the culture wars is for other people to agree with you more often, that may not get us very far.

Civil wars happen when irreconcilable differences prove impossible to resolve through peaceful political means. 'Culture wars always precede shooting wars. They don't *necessarily* lead to a shooting war, but you never have a shooting war without a culture war prior to it, because culture provides the justifications for violence', is how James Davison Hunter, the US sociologist who popularised the term 'culture wars' thirty years ago, reflected on the Washington insurgency after the last US presidential election.[1]

If the term is being used rigorously, a culture war conflict involves a clash of fundamental principles, where people feel a sense of existential threat, and the argument feels irreconcilable, because it is a deep moral clash over the identity and meaning of the nation itself, so it is not the sort of issue on which it feels possible to compromise, or to agree to disagree about. (Obviously, 'culture war' is also used much more loosely than this, to mean any argument or twitterstorm about identity.)

If culture wars are about how fundamentally different visions of the future of a nation generate existential threats, then being able to defuse or even 'call off' a culture war dynamic, on principled terms, becomes the core challenge, the test of success, of my approach to inclusive patriotism, with its effort to persuade that we could all share the society that we call home.

Clear blue water? Why not being America may not be enough

There are culture wars in America, which manage to keep escalating, year by year, and decade by decade.

Even the Covid pandemic was seen by many Americans as a party issue. Wearing a face-mask or not was almost akin to strapping a presidential ballot paper to your face. The biggest gaps on who got vaccinated were not by class or ethnic group, but by political party. Nine out of ten Democrats got a Covid vaccine, compared to slightly over half (58 per cent) of Republicans.[2] Partisan division, taken too far, costs lives. By contrast, efforts to stoke a Covid culture war in Britain proved very shallow. Eighty-three per cent of people in Britain felt it was important to take the vaccine to be a good citizen, with next to no ideological or partisan divide at all.

After Donald Trump's unfounded claims that the election was stolen, most voters for each of the two main parties now disagree about whether the presidential election was legitimate, and there are parallel narratives about the 6 January 2020 attack on the Capitol. Abortion, in both 1973 and 2022, has been an archetype of the US culture wars, contested largely as a moral imperative. The Supreme Court ruling over Roe versus Wade mobilised opponents of abortion for a generation. Its modern reversal is now mobilising women on what feels like an existential question for many Americans.

So America's bridgers and depolarisers face deep dilemmas, best described by Ezra Klein in his excellent synthesis *Why We're Polarized*, concerning how US democracy can respond to sustained polarisation.[3] There has been a reciprocal dynamic over the decades of mutual polarisation. But the threat to democratic institutions is not a 'both sides' threat. Who wins and loses the next presidential election may present starkly different scenarios for what to do next.

By America's standards, we do not have culture wars in Britain, at least not yet, especially if we take the civil war metaphor seriously, even if we are having many big arguments about identity. Yet, by British standards, we feel much more divided than we are used to, than we expect, or than we want to be. Eight out of ten people describe Britain as divided, and a broad majority say our society feels as divided as it has ever been. Most people in Britain think of themselves as balancers, and part of a society in which we respect the views of those we disagree with. This can help to foster an aversion to 'culture war' politics. Yet our politics over the last decade has not lived up to this self-image.

How Britain handled the big identity clashes of the last half-century offers grounds for confidence. Progressives and traditionalists had some big clashes about the direction and pace of social change, yet those arguments have largely resulted in new social norms. One striking illustration of this can be seen in how several of the questions that British Social Attitudes surveys used to track people's views have ceased to be important, because most social conservatives and social liberals in Britain now agree on issues that used to split people down the middle. Traditional gender roles – that it is a man's job to earn money and a woman's to look after the home – had 48 per cent to 33 per cent support in 1984, yet there was a 72 per cent to 8 per cent consensus against the same proposition by 2017. Other BSA questions – what people would feel about their children marrying across ethnic lines, or having a boss from a different ethnicity – have seen a similar shrinking back to single-digit opposition. The fastest shift came in attitudes to homosexuality. Seventy-five per cent of people thought it was always or mostly wrong in 1987, and that was still 50 per cent around the time of the millennium. Now three-quarters of people support gay marriage. British attitudes to culture and identity are increasingly liberal – because most people accept and value the social changes of the last half-century – though moderately conservative at the boundaries, many being sceptical about some of the language used to promote future more progressive and radical changes. Those with progressive views may have a high sense of jeopardy about how far these past gains are secure. But a pattern of attitudes has emerged that gives good grounds to think that a sense of mutual existential conflict can be defused, without sacrificing substantive social advances.

This makes the British 'culture war' skirmishes somewhat more temperate than the more 'bring it on' battles of France or the USA. It is more like culture war jujitsu. The aim of the British culture war often appears to be to establish that 'they' – the other side – are the culture warriors.

While Éric Zemmour was seeking to outflank Marine Le Pen in the French Presidential Election, with his advocacy of the Great Replacement Theory, and the US elections were being fought on starkly contrasting views of abortion, electoral integrity and what to teach in schools, the British culture wars appeared rather muted by comparison. When Liz Truss was Women and Equalities Minister, she gave a speech, heralded as a landmark challenge to 'the woke ideology'. It did contain some soundbites to that end, scrapping unconscious bias training as a waste of time. Yet it also contained passages, on discrimination by gender, by sexuality, that echoed the policy of the 1997 New Labour governments, as well as on the incomplete journey to equality, and the discrimination still faced by women, gay people and the disabled. Read through the eyes of an American or French culture warrior, this might have seemed a rather politically correct and almost woke-ish piece of woke-bashing, despite its rhetorical framing.

It is easy to find Labour supporters who want to call off the 'culture wars', and whose main proposal is that the Conservatives should stop using them as a political tactic. The right has the opposite perception: that it is the so-called 'woke' left that starts identity battles, over pronouns and statues, before calling Conservatives culture warriors if they disagree. Both of these narratives play well with each party's internal audience, but neither does much to help get the boundaries right.

Talking ourselves into the culture wars

Balancer Britain remains a rather middling country on both culture clashes and political polarisation. But we should not underestimate the challenges of keeping it that way.

It would be 'dangerous' to assume that this cannot take hold here, Professor Bobby Duffy tells me. Duffy and his colleagues at the Policy Institute at King's College London have probably spent more time than anybody else studying the comparative and national dynamics of culture war conflicts. He agrees that Britain is a long way from America, yet notes that America was not nearly so polarised two or three decades ago as it has become. How far the US escalation was a top-down or bottom-up process is hotly contested among researchers, but within that debate there is a broad consensus that politicians, media outlets and civic society groups did play a key role. Almost all studies emphasise the importance of political leaders trying to manage tensions. The UK has a different starting point, with less polarised public attitudes. But what the King's College research shows is that there can be an 'incredibly fast-moving dynamic' as with how quickly terms like 'woke' and 'cancel culture' have grown in awareness. The research shows that 50 per cent of people had not heard of the term 'cancel culture' in 2021 but that had halved to just a quarter within 12 months. 'We literally can talk ourselves into a culture war,' Duffy warns, and the evidence suggests that this is what we are currently doing.

It would be possible to sketch four potential scenarios for cultural conflict in Britain: that cultural conflict might largely evaporate; escalate significantly towards US levels of polarisation; become sustained and institutionalised; or be effectively defused.

An 'evaporation' scenario would see the shift away from the age of identity towards a new age of economics, where other issues – economics, energy, international politics, climate change – become sustained, with decreasing political, media or public appetite for issues of culture and identity, so much so that the 2015–22 period in which issues of identity and culture seemed dominant proves to be a blip, supporting the hypothesis that there was very little British public appetite for culture wars. This is an implausible scenario because, while there could be a significant shift towards economics, taxation and spending as the most salient public issues, there is simply too much engagement with issues of identity – particularly within political parties, among media outlets, and within academic and civic society.

A full-on culture-war scenario, where British politics and public discourse accelerate polarisation, and connect much deeper and irreconcilable clashes across a wider range of issues, is also implausible. The UK lacks the depth of social division in the US – particularly the strength of faith-based and secular worldviews, and the intensity this brings to a wide range of debates from abortion to gun control – for identity conflicts to link up across the full range of issues. However, it is possible that specific UK debates, especially around issues of race, identity and history, may see a strong US influence on both progressives and conservatives.

A more likely scenario is the normalisation of increased conflict, with a more gradual drift into increased cultural conflict. Although not reaching US levels of polarisation across the full range of social questions, our current trajectory could entrench and institutionalise a much higher level of UK polarisation in ways that could be reinforced by shifts in expectations and behaviour, and an erosion of previous informal norms, mutually justified by the claim that it is only responding in kind to the hypocrisies of our opponents.

This institutionalised conflict scenario is where the UK is currently heading. The key drivers of this are essentially the asymmetric hyper-activism of more polarising voices, especially if bridging voices are both less organised and sometimes conflict-avoidant. The hyper-activism of more polarising voices on both left and right is reflected in the media and political institutions, which shifts the incentives for MPs and political leaders.

The fourth scenario is of reduced conflict, not because issues of culture and identity evaporate and disappear, but because of active and sustained defusion strategies. Obviously, this is the desired outcome, but finding practical ways to tackle or mitigate this asymmetry of energy and mobilisation between polarisers and bridgers may be the key to challenging a drift into sustained polarisation.

How politics can weaponise and polarise patriotism

It is difficult to think of any politician chosen to govern a major democracy who did not engage with patriotism and the symbols of the country that they aspired to lead. But politicians can be as much part of the problem as the solution when it comes to the politics of patriotism.

Locating their political party as having a vision of the national story that explains their priorities and programmes, as successful leaders of different parties have done, is seen as good. But politicians promote an exclusive patriotism if they appear to claim that national symbols, like the Union Jack, belong to one party and not another. And attacks on political opponents as 'plastic patriots' or 'unpatriotic' are an attempt to narrow the authentic nation. Party politics play an important linking role for busy citizens to help make representative democracy work. But our problem is that the mobilisation of 'them and us' divides, and party politics has a strong tendency to entrench this. Party identities often thrive on affective polarisation, especially when the primary appeal becomes mistrust of the out-group, whether selfish Tories or soft-headed socialists, nationalists or unionists, Leavers or Remainers.

Sustained political polarisation on issues of identity and culture is now having a corrosive effect on national symbols and cohesion, particularly with younger people. British Future's research finds that 65 per cent of people associate the Union Jack with pride and patriotism, down from 78 per cent a decade ago. This falls to 55 per cent in Scotland, demonstrating that the Union flag is now seen very much as an indicator of a political position against independence. While Scottish identity has transcended the polarised argument about independence, the fall in seeing the Saltire (the Scottish flag) as a symbol of pride and patriotism has also fallen to 70 per cent from 84 per cent, indicating some mutual dissociation of Scotland's political tribes.[4]

Politicians can play a more positive role in an inclusive patriotism when they show more than they tell. Those on the left can help to normalise patriotism, in its inclusive form. Rather than treating their embrace of the flag as some kind of taboo-busting breakthrough, which risks just reinforcing the message that the left struggles on this territory, it would be better to demonstrate an everyday ease with national symbols that represent both tradition and modernity, from Remembrance Sunday to major royal events, national sporting events and major anniversaries.

Politicians on the right can help to normalise patriotism, in its inclusive form, when they reach out beyond their traditional support base, so that they engage across generations in particular, and emphasise a blend of modern and traditional representations of British pride. What we can ask of our political leaders is that they try to have those big democratic arguments without fanning the flames of unconstructive culture wars. They could be asked to remember that our flags, our national symbols, are things we come together around, in victory and defeat in sport and song contests, so as to engage with them while remembering that they are not the property of any political tribe, but of their fellow citizens too. Above all, we need to encourage parties to aspire to build broader coalitions, and bridge social divides, rather than to lock them in.

How to talk ourselves into a culture war anyway

If we do talk ourselves into a culture war that most people don't want, there will be three prime suspects; party politics, the media, and social media firms. Navigating identity conflict is becoming more difficult. The internet significantly amplifies polarisation, because it gives a much greater share of voice to those with the strongest views. This recurring dynamic influences national political and media actors, so that the most active, energised and mobilised further dominate debates. It is often said that the main problem on the internet is 'filter bubbles', that mean we only talk to the like-minded. That distorting effect can happen – and can present particular dangers in removing inhibitions to extremism or violence if some people are part of a 24/7 milieu in which extreme views are an unchallenged norm.

Less attention can be paid to the opposite problem: that we do encounter people with different views to our own, but are most likely to come across the strongest version of that view. We can use anecdotal examples to build a ladder of inference to confirm our own stereotype of our opponents. If meaningful contact can be a source of increased empathy and understanding of those with different views, fleeting contact can reinforce stereotypes – I knew that is what they are *really* like – especially if we don't know in everyday life people with a different view to our own.

Talking it over: how we can learn to disagree better

'Respect for the freedom of speech of others – even if you don't agree with them.' That came out on top when the public were asked to identify which British values are most important. If that is who we think we want to be, we do not seem to be doing very well at putting the ideal into practice.

As we have seen, the term 'cancel culture' became a much more familiar term to many people in 2020, but that fell to a quarter a year later. Claims and counter-claims about free speech and its boundaries have the potential to link up all of the other culture clashes in British society into a 'them and us' clash.

Most British people are balancers, not absolutists, on free speech. But it is hard to get the balances right. We often seem to over-reach in both directions.

As I sat down to watch the Disney cartoon *Aladdin* with my nine-year-old daughter, having told her that the Genie character was very funny, we were confronted with a 12-second content warning, telling us that the depictions in the film 'were wrong then and wrong now'. An identical message appears before *Dumbo*, *The Jungle Book*, *Lady and the Tramp* and *Peter Pan*. This is an upgrade on a previous message about 'outdated cultural representations'.

'Trigger warnings' have become a contentious topic. Yet rigorous efforts to test their influence has found how little difference they make, beyond some mild unintended consequences. They appear to slightly increase anxiety when the warning itself is shown, but with no discernible impact on how the questionable content itself is received.[5] It seems that much less harm or good is done than either critics or advocates suggest. But my worry is that liberals underestimate the reputational damage of over-policing harmless harms. I think it sends the message that all of the serious stuff has been sorted out if there is time to engage on these boundaries. Yet at around the same time that I was being mildly irked by the Disney Channel's warning, I was receiving more racist abuse than at any other point in my life, due to the under-policing of incessant abuse and hatred by major social media platforms. So my sense is that we can get this wrong in both directions.

One of the best ways to deal with the fear of not being able to talk about a subject is to talk it through. So I began experimenting with a methodology for engaging with people who have concerns about free speech. Across the two long summers of the pandemic, I spent large chunks of time putting that theory to the test: holding 50 group discussions on Zoom so people could talk through the topics they didn't think were talked about enough. The twist was to meet up with the same people three times, each time a fortnight apart, to talk through which issue the group thought might be the most difficult. So we reconvened to talk about race and racism, history and statues, immigration and asylum seekers, Brexit, political correctness, Covid, free speech online, crime and anti-social behaviour, the benefits system, shifting views of sexuality, trans rights, and how to decide what you could and couldn't trust in the media, or on the internet.

Invariably, the participants found the experience positive, cathartic and reassuring. Many said at the end that they felt quite cagey at the start – was this emphasis on giving your honest opinion really genuine? – but that changed over time.

I found several things reassuring about these conversations. Though participants, by design, had tougher views than average, they saw themselves as balancers too. The commonplace observation that political correctness could go a bit too far very often now came with the caveat that it probably had a point in the first place, with no nostalgia or regret about the loss of mocking terms for gay people or ethnic minorities that had often still been seen as banter in the 1970s or 1980s. Generational change was a recurring theme. Older participants often talked about having different views to their own parents (described as old-fashioned or closed-minded on homosexuality or race) and to their children, who might be challenging their grandparents on what you should say and how to say it. Almost everyone thought that what they tended to call 'live and let live' attitudes to gay people marked progress: so many people could cite gay relatives, colleagues, or friends of friends, who only first got the chance to get married in later life. But they still wondered how to keep up with the number of genders that young people said existed these days.

There were widely shared common-sense intuitions about how to get the boundaries right. A typical comment was: 'I think sometimes people are ready to jump down your throat too quickly. They should wait until you have been racist before they call you a racist. Maybe you just have a difference of view. But then, if you do start being racist, fair enough, call that out.' There might be different perceptions, across generations, about exactly what does and does not cross that line, but it sounded like a starting point that many people could work with. There was much more confidence about how to draw that line on the now familiar topic of race, and uncertainty about what seemed a much newer discussion concerning trans rights.

Over 75 hours of 'difficult conversations' I felt the foundational boundaries did get crossed, perhaps half a dozen times. Yet other participants proved effective at challenging those examples, explaining what they felt the right or wrong way might be to make a fair point – maybe about anti-social behaviour or how integration is going – while arguing against stereotyping whole groups of people.

Almost everyone who took part felt this sort of thing should be happening much more often, but did not know where it would happen. Where local initiatives in this spirit did exist, they were not on the radar of those we met. Many people said that what they would find really interesting would be to talk to people with almost the completely opposite view to their own, and to see if civil disagreement was possible there too. I was struck by the sincerity of the appetite for trying to talk things over, for learning more, and getting back to at least disagreeing well – while not being sure where that could happen.

What can be done? A practical agenda to defuse the culture wars

The key challenge is that it seems much easier to talk our way into cultural conflict than to talk our way out of it. An effort to defuse culture wars involves both swimming with the tide of what most people want, and at the same time swimming against the online, media and political culture that we have developed. Here is my mini-manifesto for some practical ways we could seek to shift that.

(1) Avoidance doesn't work

If you want to help to call off and defuse the culture wars, then don't try to stay out of them! Declaring that nobody cares, so it won't happen here, will not do much to defuse culture war dynamics in Britain. The intuition that most British people are too sensible to want perpetual cultural conflicts to dominate our public discourse is probably true. But it won't be enough to keep our heads down, cross our fingers and hope that efforts to stoke 'culture wars' will fail and go away.

The fatal flaw of an 'avoidance' approach to reducing the temperature is that its most likely effect is to simply concede more space for the most polarising voices.

Issues of identity are not a 'distraction' from 'real issues'. Issues of identity are meaningful to most of us. Of course, there are many other substantive issues – war and peace, taxation and public services, the cost of living, and many others. But it is difficult to find many people who genuinely do not care about identity, culture or symbolism at all. If you are in the minority of those who really don't care about the monarchy, for example, or whether we keep statues, or put any new ones up, you may still have views about those who boo when footballers take the knee, or what should and should not be taught in schools about faith, tolerance or history.

It is good to remind everybody, including ourselves, that we do not need to jump into the trenches to debate every piece of clickbait on the internet. But an avoidance strategy fails to differentiate between trivia and substance. Defusing culture wars depends on proactive engagement with the substance of issues of identity and culture. On issues like history; race and fairness; gender and sexuality, especially if, as most of us do, we care about how our society tries to get the outcomes right, while also seeking to contain unconstructive conflict and polarisation.

(2) Mind our language: we can turn down the temperature

If we want to resist the culture war dynamics, we should be wary of 'meta-identities', which seek to join up every identity issue into one giant clash about everything.

We could reduce the temperature by talking more about identity clashes and cultural arguments, and less about 'culture wars'. There are far fewer guns in Britain than in America, partly thanks to the decisions made after the Dunblane massacre in 1996. That can mitigate how far angry rhetoric during heightened times might socialise some of those on the fringes into violence. Jo Cox MP was murdered in June 2016 by a man with far-right views, and Sir David Amess in 2022 by an extreme Islamist. Many more MPs have received threats or had to increase security measures.

The case for desisting from the use of the language of enemies and traitors in politics concerns not simply the dangers of violence from the most angry, but also a broader point about the public culture we should want.

It would also be better to use the term 'culture warrior' much more sparingly. This pejorative term should be reserved for cynical and bad-faith efforts to stoke up symbolic issues, rather than being extended to any progressive or conservative engagement with issues of identity and culture. Stereotyping, of the 'woke' and the 'snowflakes' or those on the other flank, may be part of free debate, but we should proactively encourage those who want to get beyond name-calling to engage with the substance of what is at stake.

(3) Value the institutions that we share – especially the BBC

Where we have institutions that bring us together, we should value and protect them. We need to share things in common to find a sense of solidarity, despite the things that divide us. An important difference between Britain and America is our greater number of shared institutions that transcend social and political divides: the NHS, the monarchy, Remembrance and the Armed Forces, our sporting teams – all do this.

Yet the danger of an era of ever-increasing polarisation is that, if the itch to turn everything into new ammunition for the identity wars proves irresistible, then national institutions and occasions become attractive targets for cultural conflict.

The institutions that could help us reach across our divides may be those most in danger of becoming embroiled in the next culture war. The BBC may be both most vulnerable to this dynamic and the institution that it matters most that we protect. Losing the BBC would take us one big step closer to US-style dystopia, where two partisan tribes consume the nightly news in two parallel universes. This has implications for how its supporters might seek to protect the BBC. A 'progressive campaign' to save the BBC could be as much part of the problem as the solution by deepening the sense that it is an issue of partisan contention. So a sustained and sustainable coalition for the BBC would need to transcend social and political tribes, rather than becoming a marker of identification between them. It would need to try to rise above the so-called 'culture wars' and seek instead to become a significant site of meaningful dialogue concerning issues of substance (rather than trivia) contested within them.

(4) Get the boundaries right on free speech and hate speech

We need a more serious and granular debate about free speech, which moves from 'sides' and slogans to 'solutions'. The 'left' of this debate would do well to stop over-policing trivia, and to place more emphasis on setting out what should be permitted and protected, before drawing the line. The 'right' of this debate should set out what it is legitimate to exclude.

A serious and more granular debate about the foundations and the boundaries would make some important gains. It would reveal where there is already a significant latent consensus beneath the sloganising. It would illuminate which areas are substantively contested, and why, so enabling a more focused debate.

This would help to create clarity about what should be excluded by law (violence, intimidation, abuse and threat); what legal content should be legitimately stigmatised and excluded from mainstream institutions even though it may be legal speech (overt racism; discrimination that denies the rights and equal status of others); and what should be promoted not by rules but by cultural change. A good vision is to have conversations about

out-groups that would continue in the presence of a member of that group.

I would propose defending the right to offend, but not the right to dehumanise. So I agree with Lord Justice Sedley, when he said in an important 1999 test case, 'Free speech includes not only the inoffensive but the irritating, the contentious, the eccentric, the heretical, the unwelcome and the provocative provided it does not tend to provoke violence.'[6] Those are good adjectives to define what should be permitted. I would also look through the other end of the telescope, and add that while free speech does include the contentious and the provocative, could we also agree that it should exclude the abusive, the intimidatory and the dehumanising?

That distinction seems to me to catch the type of ostensibly non-violent extremism and hatred that socialises people towards violence. Those who worry about 'legal but harmful' content being excluded would invariably want to exclude legal but harmful content from some mainstream institutions and platforms. For example, 'the Jews/Muslims are vermin' is legal but harmful speech that almost nobody would propose to protect. I think there would be a broad consensus for excluding Holocaust denial, and for stigmatising and often excluding discriminatory statements such as 'no blacks in our team', 'no women in maths and science' or 'never trust the Muslims and Jews: they are out to destroy us all'.

There is a stronger latent consensus than we think on free speech, but getting the foundations right is essential if we are to then call for people to 'disagree well'. We need to focus less on cancellation and more on how positive change happens. That means creating more of the missing spaces for meaningful dialogue about how to get the boundaries right in different specific contexts – from educational settings, to civic and political institutions, to comedy and entertainment, to what rules and expectations we might set for online forums, to what efforts we can all make to promote broader cultural changes.

(5) Take responsibility. Identify the roles that each of us can play in bridging divides and promoting meaningful dialogue

The primary challenge is that it is much easier to talk ourselves into a culture war than to talk ourselves out of one. Some voices are louder than others. So our politicians, our broadcasters and our newspapers play a big role in making the weather for the rest of us. It matters a great deal to the public climate how far politicians and political parties decide to be amplifiers or diffusers of cultural conflict. It would make a decisive difference if political leaders tried to build bridges. They do have some incentives to broaden their electoral coalitions. But they may also have incentives to reinforce the 'them and us' perceptions of 35 per cent or 40 per cent of the country, so as to energise and mobilise their own base. So we cannot rely on political leaders trying to bring us together (although it would help if they were to try). Elections and referendums divide, and ask us to take a side. But both progressive and conservative politicians can decide to be navigators of culture and identity dialogues, without resiling from their own right and responsibility to take a position.

The King could play an important role in championing an inclusive patriotism. As well as honouring his own oaths and pledges to serve his citizens of every colour and creed, the King could ask each of us to consider what we can do, practically, to make our contribution to an era of renewal and reconnection.

Governments can help the rest of society to connect if they put some of the basics in place. We need universal fluency in a shared language for everybody who settles here. Schools that are mixed, not segregated. Places near us where we can meet and mix.

How far politicians stoke and exploit divisions, or seek to bridge them, can make an important difference. But, whatever politicians decide, every institution, and every individual, can play some part in the decisions we make about when to avoid, how to fight, and on what terms we can defuse 'culture war' conflicts.

After all, it is not just the leaders of political parties, movements and causes but their followers who set social norms. Messengers matter in reinforcing social norms: a twitterstorm of challenges that come solely from opponents will often lead to a defensive reaction of doubling down. Challenging opponents is part of political advocacy – to score points. Challenging friends is harder. Partisan perceptions are powerful. People will quickly see their opponents' behaviour as unforgivably egregious, even when clumsy rather than malign, while being more likely to mitigate the behaviour of allies.

So those within a faith group, a social tribe or a political family have a particular value in reinforcing norms and boundaries. Protecting social norms is fundamentally about the willingness to apply standards within your own political 'tribe' that you demand of the rival tribes. I would like to see more of us make a concerted effort to encourage that as a civic social norm – to recognise and boost the reputational capital of those who do this, and to notice too those who always put their party and cause above that principle of fair play.

There are different challenges for progressive and conservative movements. Progressive civil society would favour reducing the temperature in principle, but would mostly see the fault as lying elsewhere, since its own causes are righteous. Mobilising support without creating 'them and us' polarisation may be challenging, yet there are significant long-term gains for causes that can broaden their geographic reach by building stronger coalitions across social class, educational and political divides.

Meanwhile, conservative institutions and movements face choices too. There is a difference between scrutinising and challenging proposals for change and making a deliberate effort to amplify fringe voices in order to create a heightened sense of cultural conflict. There can be short-term incentives to do this – for politicians, or for media outlets – but it is to the long-term detriment of mainstream conservatism to artificially amplify cultural conflict in society, especially if it becomes unable to reach across generations.

Where we are missing places and spaces of meaningful connection and contact in which we can engage with those who are not like us, we should create more of them. Intermediate institutions have a big role to play, particularly in providing the spaces for meaningful contact over specific issues and in helping to reduce the social distance between people, bridging divides of education and class, geography and ethnicity – but having the reach to do this well is a challenge. The point of civil society is to mediate, but civil society cannot mediate if it does not have the relationships that reach across key social divides. Many civil society organisations may need to work at being less narrow – on both ethnic diversity and social class, and to reach across geographic and educational divides – to develop more potential for the type of meaningful contact that challenges polarisation.

We should look to our great universities to be as locally rooted as they are globally engaged, so that they are places that seek to reach across the educational, geographic and generation gaps in our debates about identity, rather than articulating only one pole of the arguments.

We should ask every school to educate for a shared society, so no child goes to school in Britain without meaningful contact across race and ethnicity, social class and the local geography. Much of what we can do to build connections is up to us, as citizens.

Every institution in our society can play a relevant role in achieving this. We can make small, significant differences every day, in our personal interactions on the internet, as well as in the real world. Calling off a culture war is not something any of us can do on our own. Yet we can each use our voice and power to play our part.

Conclusion

The New Patriotism That We Need

We each have different journeys to being British. Some of you can trace your ancestors back beyond the first Kings of England and of Scotland being crowned over a thousand years ago, or from before the three centuries of this United Kingdom.

Some of us are the first, second or third generations of Britons who became part of this island story in the three-quarters of a century since the *Empire Windrush* docked at Tilbury in 1948. Yet that was just one chapter in a much longer story of three centuries of Empire and decolonisation, of wartime service and sacrifice. It is no coincidence that the 75th birthday of the National Health Service, the jewel in the new crown of our post-war welfare settlement, follows just a fortnight later, so inextricably linked have been those stories of migration, of integration, and the NHS.

I am a child of our NHS as much as a child of Britain after Empire, the son of an Indian doctor and an Irish nurse among so many who came to this country – among hundreds and thousands who contributed their care and service to the best exemplar of how the diversity of modern Britain has made a foundational contribution to something we all benefit from.

This has been a book about 'them and us' – about the many arguments concerning identity that can divide us in a democratic society. It has been about Evertonians and Liverpudlians, about migrants and hosts, about minorities and majorities, about the English and the Scots, the Welsh and the Irish, about Catholics and Protestants, Nationalists and Unionists, Jews and Muslims, Monarchists and Republicans, Remainers and Leavers, liberals and traditionalists, right and left – about the arguments we have, and what we must try to do to navigate those differences if we are to live together. But it has also been a book about how we, the British, became us, the people we are today and what we can learn from how people become us – about what we could choose to do together if we do not want our society to be defined by our differences.

Do we need patriotism to help us to do that? It may look to many people as though patriotism could be part of the problem, especially in a multi-national as well as multi-ethnic and multi-faith society. There will be competing patriotisms across the nations of Britain. There will be different ideas and arguments about what each of them mean.

But I don't believe we become a more inclusive society by dispensing with patriotism – by putting flags, anthems and national occasions aside. I think we would then risk giving up some of the occasions that can be important in reminding us that our differences need not define us.

In a democratic and individualistic society, this could only be a patriotism of attraction and persuasion, not compulsion and coercion. When we do things together it will be because we choose to, and will be more powerful because it is voluntary. Rather, we should make sure that everybody is invited to the party, and can have a voice in what we want our symbols and flags to represent today. But I want us to avoid making the mistake of thinking that we make patriotism more inclusive by taking and thinning things out.

An inclusive patriotism can celebrate most of the things that we cherish from our past and present. We can take enormous pride in the culture that is our lucky inheritance if we are British – the language and literature from Shakespeare, infused by the Irish and Commonwealth contributions, our sense of place in these islands, the songs and the sports that we share.

We can have a shared cultural patriotism, when we see the power of attraction of our culture to those who become British is a vote of confidence in our culture and traditions, not a dilution or threat, while those who join our club can help to write the next chapters. We can and should choose to be the country that puts most energy and effort into celebrating those who join our society and choose to become British – and to make English and Scottish, Welsh and Northern Irish identities something that everybody who comes to call those nations their home are invited to participate in too.

A confident patriotism would be able to handle the complexity of the past that has made us the society that we are today, wanting to hear all of the voices and stories about how we got here. That should not mean replacing one monolithic story with another, but understanding the journeys that brought us to our common home.

What is the patriotism that we need in times like these? In its essence, patriotism is a love of country, and a sense of belonging to it. If we want to get beyond 'them and us', we need the patriotisms that are willing to work with the both/and, and that are interested in how the story of the 'new us' that we have become goes next.

I don't think you can be much of a patriot in Britain today if you hate the society that we have become, rather than wanting us all to make it work together.

The United Kingdom is unusual – a multi-national polity where most people identify with more than one flag, and more than one national identity. A patriotism of both/and would try to see that as an opportunity and not a threat. So I hope that we can maintain a both/and multi-national patriotism that treats the fact that most people in Britain identify with more than one flag as an opportunity, rather than suggesting we would be more authentic if we chose only one. That is not up to me. This somewhat dis-United Kingdom has become more fractious. It is undoubtedly a Union of consent. It will stay together as a political community only if that is what most people in each of Scotland, England, Wales and Northern Ireland want, or decide that they can live with.

A both/and patriotism can understand that disagreement and dissonance is part of the privilege of being a democracy, but it would see the value in defusing unconstructive 'culture war' conflicts that generate mutual animosity and fear rather than trust. We must not stop debating identity issues where we disagree, but we should also put more effort into how we could talk ourselves out of cultural conflict as well as into it. On a good day, I do feel that this is what most of us want, but it can be hard for the bridgers and the balancers to get a hearing in noisy and polarised times.

I am an optimist about Britain, by experience as well as instinct. I can see our story of this modern Britain, three-quarters of a century in, as one in which our glass can seem three-quarters full, on a good day at least, though that would still leave much more to do if we want it to be brimful and overflowing another quarter of a century from here. Our experiences may differ in sixty million or more different ways. For those of you who may think my confidence displays too much of an optimistic bias about Britain, and see the glass as still half empty, I have the same question that I have for us all: if we are starting from here, now, can we imagine again a future that we want to share?

Notes

Chapter 1

1. Kōkuto Shūsui, 'Imperalism', reproduced in Robert Thomas Tierney, *Monster of the Twentieth Century: Kotoku Shusui and Japan's First Anti-Imperialist Movement*, 1st edn (University of California Press, 2015).
2. Albert Camus in *France Football*, 17 July 1957.
3. Dan Fisher, 'Split Between Britain, U.S. Seen as "Inevitable": The Conservative Party Chairman Fears that a "Less European" America will Provide the Wedge', *Los Angeles Times*, 19 April 1990; https://www.latimes.com/archives/la-xpm-1990-04-19-mn-2009-story.html
4. E. J. Hobsbawm, *Nations and Nationalism since 1780: Programme, Myth, Reality*, 2nd edn (Cambridge University Press, 1992).
5. Y. Mounk, *The Great Experiment: How to Make Diverse Democracies Work* (Bloomsbury, 2022).

Chapter 2

1. Enoch Powell, Speech to London Rotary Club, Eastbourne, 16 November 1968. This speech, in which Powell replies to critics of his more famous Birmingham 'Rivers of Blood' speech, seven months earlier, often articulates his argument more clearly.
2. Powell, Birmingham speech, 20 April 1968.
3. Enoch Powell, 'Patriotism', sermon to the St Lawrence Jewry in the City of London (18 January 1977), quoted in Simon Heffer, *Like the Roman: The Life of Enoch Powell* (Weidenfeld & Nicolson, 1998).
4. Camilla Schofield, *Enoch Powell and the Making of Postcolonial Britain* (Cambridge University Press, 2013).
5. Lenny Henry, *Who Am I Again?* (Faber, 2019).

6. Matthew Parris, 'A Lexicon of Conservative Cant', *The Spectator*, 19 February 2000; https://www.spectator.co.uk/article/from-the-archives-are-you-politically-sound/

7. Simon Heffer, *Like the Roman: The Life of Enoch Powell* (Weidenfeld & Nicolson, 1998).

8. Ibid.

9. Humphry Berkeley, *The Odyssey of Enoch: A Political Memoir* (Hamish Hamilton, 1977).

10. Enoch Powell, Speech to The Royal Society of St George in London, 23 April 1961.

11. Enoch Powell, St George's Day speech, 1961.

12. Enoch Powell, speech at Trinity College, Dublin, 1964; quoted in Bernard Porter, *The Absent-Minded Imperialists: Empire, Society, and Culture in Britain* (Oxford University Press, 2006), in Robert Saunders, *Yes to Europe* (Cambridge University Press, 2018) and in Robert Saunders, 'Myths from a Small Island', *New Statesman*, October 2019; https://www.newstatesman.com/politics/2019/10/myths-from-a-small-island-the-dangers-of-a-buccaneering-view-of-british-history

13. Robert Moore earlier uses it as a chapter title in his 1975 book, *Racism and Black Resistance in Britain* (Pluto, 1975), attributing the phrase to a Sri Lankan friend, presumably Sivanandan. I am grateful to Edward Anderson of Northumbria University for this reference.

14. Ian Sanjay Patel, *'We're Here Because You Were There': Immigration and the End of Empire* (Verso, 2021).

15. David Olusoga, 'The toppling of Edward Colston's statue is not an attack on history. It is history', *The Guardian*, 8 June 2020; https://www.guardian.com/commentisfree/2020/jun/08/edward-colston-statue-history-slave-trader-bristol-protest

16. Tristran Cork, 'Edward Colston statue: Society of Merchant Venturers respond', *Bristol Post*, 8 June 2020; https://www.bristolpost.co.uk/news/bristol-news/edward-colston-statue-society-merchant-4203544

17. John Lloyd, 'Enlightened advocate, or the great delayer? Henry Dundas's complex relationship with slavery', *Prospect*, March 2022; https://www.prospectmagazine.co.uk/society-and-culture/henry-dundas-slavery-statues-blm-edinburgh-scotland

18. Quoted in Lloyd, 'Enlightened advocate or the great delayer?'

19. Akala, *Natives: Race and Class in the Ruins of Empire* (Two Roads, 2018).

Notes

Chapter 3

1. I am grateful to Frank Sharry, founder of America's Voice in the USA, for introducing me to this encapsulation of the framing of anti-migration narratives.
2. Cassilde Schwartz, et al., 'A Populist Paradox? How Brexit Softened Anti-Immigrant Attitudes', *British Journal of Political Science*, 51(3) (2021), 1160–80.
3. S. Blinder, 'Imagined Immigration: The Impact of Different Meanings of "Immigrants" in Public Opinion and Policy Debates in Britain', *Political Studies*, 63(1) (2015), 80–100.
4. Daisuke Akimoto, 'Japan's Changing Immigration and Refugee Policy', *The Diplomat* (March 2021); https://thediplomat.com/2021/03/japans-changing-immigration-and-refugee-policy/
5. P. Gatrell, *The Unsettling of Europe: How Migration Reshaped a Continent* (Basic Books, 2019).
6. Max Frisch, 'Over-foreignisation', 1965 preface to Siamo Italiano; 1966 lecture; https://publikationen.ub.uni-frankfurt.de/frontdoor/index/index/year/2010/docId/14072. For the origins of the phrase discussed in 'we wanted workers but we got people instead', see Mark Krikorian, *National Review*, February 2016; https://www.nationalreview.com/corner/george-borjas-immigration-blog/
7. Anuscheh Farahat and Kay Hailbronner, 'Report on Citizenship Law: Germany' (European University Institute, March 2020); https://cadmus.eui.eu/bitstream/handle/1814/66430/RSCAS_GLOBALCIT_CR_2020_5.pdf?sequence=1
8. *The Economist* and Anne Wroe, *The Economist Style Guide*, 12th edn (Economist Books, 2018).

Chapter 4

1. David Cannadine, 'The Context, Performance and Meaning of Ritual: The British Monarchy and the "Invention of Tradition", c. 1820–1977', in E. Hobsbawm and T. Ranger, *The Invention of Tradition* (Cambridge University Press, 2012), 101–64.
2. Walter Bagehot, *The English Constitution* (1867), Cambridge Texts (2001).
3. George Orwell, *The Lion and the Unicorn: Socialism and the English Genius* (Secker & Warburg, 1941).
4. Robert Worcester, 'Reflections on the Impact of the Death of Diana on The Monarchy' (Ipsos-Mori, August 2007).
5. Clement Attlee, 'From Victorian to Elizabethan: The Role of the Monarchy', reproduced in Frank Field (ed.), *Attlee's Great Contemporaries: The Politics of Character* (Bloomsbury, 2009).

6. A. Blick and P. Hennessy, 'Good Chaps No More? Safeguarding the Constitution in Stressful Times' (Constitution Society, 2019); https://consoc.org.uk/wp-content/uploads/2019/11/FINAL-Blick-Hennessy-Good-Chaps-No-More.pdf
7. Powell, quoted in Philip Murphy, '"On Her Own": The Queen and the Commonwealth in the 1980s', in *Monarchy and the End of Empire: The House of Windsor, the British Government, and the Postwar Commonwealth* (Oxford Academic, 2014), Chapter 10.

Chapter 5

1. Brian Cathcart, *The Case of Stephen Lawrence* (Viking, 1999).
2. Hashi Mohamed, 'Sir William Macpherson on what has happened since he led the inquiry into Stephen Lawrence's muder', *The Times*, 11 March 2019; https://www.thetimes.co.uk/article/sir-william-macpherson-on-what-has-happened-since-he-led-theinquiry-into-stephen-lawrences-murder-bbdpb3kdb
3. Ibid.
4. Doreen Lawrence, *And Still I Rise: A Mother's Search for Justice* (Faber & Faber, 2011).
5. Duwayne Brooks, *Steve and Me: My Friendship with Stephen Lawrence and the Quest for Justice* (Brooks Books, 2006).
6. Barbara Cohen, 'The Stephen Lawrence Inquiry Report: 20 years On' (Runnymede Trust); https://assets.website-files.com/61488f992b58e687f1108c7c/61c3137609bff8656ca03761_StephenLawrence20briefing.pdf
7. Baroness Casey, 'The Baroness Casey Review'; https://www.crestadvisory.com/baroness-casey-review-final-report.
8. Sir William Macpherson, 'The Stephen Lawrence Inquiry Report': Cm-4261-I, 1999.
9. Macpherson: The Stephen Lawrence Inquiry Report (1999).
10. Kathy Marks, 'Lawrence Suspects Caught on Film', *The Independent*, 15 June 1998; 'Stephen Lawrence Trial: Race threats just "banter" says accused', *Evening Standard*, 12 April 2012.

Chapter 6

1. Tebbit, quoted in Kenan Malik, *From Fatwa to Jihad: How the World Changed* (Atlantic Books).
2. 'I would not shed a tear if some British Muslims, deploring his manners, should waylay him in a dark street and seek to improve them. If that should cause him thereafter to control his pen, society would benefit and literature would not suffer.'
3. Keith Vaz, 'It's the author who holds all the cards', *The Guardian*, February 1990.

4. Tariq Modood, 'On Britishness', *Fabian Review*, December 2005 (Fabian Society).
5. Sadiq Khan, 'Fairness not favours: How to reconnect with British Muslims' (Fabian Society, September 2008); https://fabians.org.uk/publication/fairness-not-favours/
6. Dr Timothy Winter, 'Finding an English Islam', Woking Peace Garden, September 2016, published by British Future; https://www.britishfuture.org/15300/
7. Burhan Wazir, 'The majority of British Muslims believe that life in the UK is better than it was five years ago', Hyphen online, 17 June 2022; https://hyphenonline.com/2022/06/17/majority-of-british-muslims-believe-that-life-in-the-uk-is-better-than-it-was-five-years-ago/; ComResSavanta: Hyphen UK Muslim attitudes survey, June 2022; https://savanta.com/knowledge-centre/poll/hyphen-uk-muslim-attitudes-survey/
8. Roy Jenkins, 'Address by the Home Secretary to the Institute of Race Relations', *Race*, 8(3) (1967), pp. 215–21; https://doi.org/10.1177/030639686700800301
9. Yasmin Alibhai-Brown, 'After Multiculturalism' (Foreign Policy Centre, 2000); https://fpc.org.uk/publications/after-multiculturalism/
10. Commission on the Future of Multi-ethnic Britain, *The Future of Multi-ethnic Britain* (Runnymede Trust/Profile Books, 2000).
11. The King's remarks to faith leaders, 16 September 2022; https://www.royal.uk/kings-remarks-faith-leaders

Chapter 7

1. 'Do you think it was right or wrong for David Cameron to hold a referendum on Britain's membership of the EU?' (What UK Thinks); https://whatukthinks.org/eu/questions/do-you-think-it-was-right-or-wrong-for-david-cameron-to-hold-a-referendum-on-britains-membership-of-the-eu/
2. 'The vote to leave the EU: Litmus test or lightning rod?', British Social Attitudes; https://www.bsa.natcen.ac.uk/media/39149/bsa34_brexit_final.pdf
3. Kirby Swales, 'Understanding the Leave vote' (National Centre for Social Research, 2017); https://whatukthinks.org/eu/analysis/understanding-the-leave-vote/
4. Rachel Ormston, *Do we feel European and does it matter?* (NatCen Social Research/UK in a Changing Europe, 2015) https://whatukthinks.org/eu/analysis/do-we-feel-european-and-does-it-matter/

5. Soames, quoted in Vernon Bogdanor, 'Learning from history: The 1975 referendum on Europe', a lecture given at Gresham College, 2016.
6. Quoted in Tim Shipman, *All Out War: The Full Story of How Brexit Sank Britain's Political Class*, (William Collins, 2016).
7. Lord Ashcroft, 'How the United Kingdom Voted on Thursday … and Why' (Lord Ashcroft Polls, 24 June 2016); https://lordashcroftpolls.com/2016/06/how-the-united-kingdom-voted-and-why/
8. M. Sobolewska and R. Ford, *Brexitland: Identity, Diversity and the Reshaping of British Politics* (Cambridge University Press, 2020).
9. P. Toynbee, 'Time to march: Because now it's the Brexiteers who are afraid', *The Guardian*, 5 June 2018; https://www.theguardian.com/commentisfree/2018/jun/05/march-brexiters-afraid-remain-peoples-will-vote

Chapter 8

1. Yasmin Alibhai-Brown and Anne Montague, *The Colour of Love: Mixed Race Relationships* (Virago, 1992); Yasmin Alibhai-Brown: *Mixed Feelings: The Complex Lives of Mixed Race Britons* (Women's Press, 2001); Remi Adekoya, *Biracial Britain: A Different Way of Looking at Race* (Constable, 2021); Kamal Ahmed. *The Life and Times of a Very British Man* (Bloomsbury, 2018).
2. Gary Younge: 'Beige Britain: a new race, officially recognised – welcome to the mixed race future' (*The Guardian*, G2 cover story, 22 May 1997).
3. Personal comment to the author, cited in Remi Adekoya, *Biracial Britain: A Different Way of Looking at Race* (Constable, 2021).
4. Tariq Modood, 'Political Blackness and British Asians', *Sociology*, 28(4) (1994), 859–76. *JSTOR*; https://www.jstor.org/stable/42857773
5. Sunder Katwala, 'The race for recognition: Lessons from the pandemic for race equality', in K. McNeill and R. Harding (eds), *Our Other National Debt* (Our Other National Debt project, 2020); https://static1.squarespace.com/static/5ea9e247aa6f 8130e910c6f0/t/5eb32ea6a1028e157d918194/1588801192519/ Our+Other+National+Debt+-+Full+Report+May+2020.pdf
6. Three per cent of ethnic minorities reported attending protests in person, while 26 per cent reported voicing support online; the comparable figures were 3 per cent and 14 per cent for white British respondents. Number Cruncher Politics for British Future, fieldwork 9–17 October 2020, reported in *Race and Opportunity in Britain: Finding Common Ground* (British Future, 2021).

7. British Future, *Race and Opportunity in Britain: Finding Common Ground*, 2021; https://www.britishfuture.org/publication/race-and-opportunity-in-britain-finding-common-ground/
8. YouGov, survey of 1270 ethnic minority adults in Great Britain, conducted 10–17 June 2020; https://yougov.co.uk/topics/politics/articles-reports/2020/06/26/nine-ten-bame-britons-think-racism-exists-same-lev and https://docs.cdn.yougov.com/6pg6w1fadp/YouGov%20Racism%20BAME%20June%202020%202.pdf
9. Ibid.
10. Commission on Race and Ethnic Disparities, *The Report of the Commission on Race and Ethnic Disparities* (March 2021).
11. Bernard Crick, 'Shaw as political thinker, or the dogs that did not bark', *Shaw*, vol. 11, (1991), 21-36.
12. Michael Holroyd, *Bernard Shaw* (Vintage, 1998).

Chapter 9

1. *The Westminster Hour*, 10 May 2014, still available online on the BBC website; https://www.bbc.co.uk/programmes/b042z1fj
2. Rishi Sunak and Saratha Rajeswaran, 'A Portrait of Modern Britain' (Policy Exchange, 2014); https://policyexchange.org.uk/publication/a-portrait-of-modern-britain/
3. Jasper King, 'Rishi Sunak's rise to PM is "Obama moment for British Hindus"', *Metro*, 24 October 2022; https://metro.co.uk/2022/10/24/southampton-hindu-temple-leader-says-rishi-sunak-our-obama-moment-17626842/
4. Charles Moore, *Margaret Thatcher: The Authorized Biography*, Vol. 3 (2019).
5. *Sunday Times* Rich List 2022, 26 October 2022; https://www.thetimes.co.uk/article/rishi-sunak-akshata-murty-net-worth-sunday-times-rich-list-86ls8n09h
6. Steven Fisher, in Philip Cowley and Dennis Kavanagh, *The British General Election of 2017* (Macmillan).
7. Benjamin Disraeli, *Sybil* (1845).

Chapter 10

1. Bernard Crick, 'The Four Nations: Interrelations' (Twenty-fifth John P. Mackintosh memorial lecture; University of Edinburgh, October 2007); https://www.ed.ac.uk/sites/default/files/atoms/files/bernardcricklecture.pdf
2. Bernard Crick, 'An Englishman Considers His Passport', *The Irish Review*, no. 5 (1988), 1–10; https://doi.org/10.2307/29735375
3. Quoted in Michael Holroyd, *Bernard Shaw* (Vintage, 1998).

4. David Trimble, Nobel Lecture, 1998; https://www.nobelprize.org/prizes/peace/1998/trimble/lecture/
5. Iain McLean and Alistair McMillan, '1707 and 1800: A Treaty (Mostly) Honoured and a Treaty Broken', Chapter 3 in *What's Wrong with the British Constitution?* (Oxford University Press, 2012).
6. Lindsay Paterson, *The Autonomy of Modern Scotland*, Edinburgh University Press (1994).
7. Quoted in the *Daily Record*, David Clegg, 26 March 2015; https://www.dailyrecord.co.uk/news/politics/independence-referendum-figures-revealed-majority-5408163
8. Stephen Noon interview with *The Times*, 27 August 2022; https://www.thetimes.co.uk/article/brains-behind-2014-yes-campaign-returns-from-life-with-the-jesuits-gchwtdjz7
9. R. Wyn Jones and J. Larner, 'Progressive Home Rule?' *IPPR Progressive Review*, 27 (3) (2020), 235–45; https://doi.org/10.1111/newe.12221

Chapter 11
1. Jack Stanton, 'How the Culture War could break democracy' *Politico* (2021); https://www.politico.com/news/magazine/2021/05/20/culture-war-politics-2021-democracy-analysis-489900
2. William Galston, 'For COVID-19 vaccinations, party affiliation matters more than race and ethnicity', *Brookings* (2021); https://www.brookings.edu/blog/fixgov/2021/10/01/for-covid-19-vaccinations-party-affiliation-matters-more-than-race-and-ethnicity/
3. Klein, E., *Why We're Polarized* (Profile Books, 2020).
4. British Future, 'Jubilee Britain: After a decade of upheaval, where are we going now?' (2022); https://www.britishfuture.org/publication/jubilee-britain/
5. Victoria Bridgland, Payton J. Jones and Benjamin W. Bellet, 'A Meta-analysis of the Effects of Trigger Warnings, Content Warnings, and Content Notes.' *OSF Preprints*, (23 August 2022); https://osf.io/qav9m/
6. Reported in *The Guardian* (24 July 1999), 'Preacher wins freedom of speech'; https://www.theguardian.com/uk/1999/jul/24/johnezard

Acknowledgements

This is my first book so its ideas have been shaped by the support of many people, who will often recognise where my thinking and writing reflects our conversations about national identity, often our collaborations and shared efforts to bridge the divides, and sometimes our (mostly) constructive disagreements about the identity clashes of these volatile times.

So, thank you for that friendly encouragement and critical engagement to David Aaronovitch, Remi Adekoya, Akeela Ahmed, Kamal Ahmed, Sughra Ahmed, Vidhya Alakeson, Yasmin Alibhai-Brown, Andrea Als, Qari Asim, Olivia Bailey, Steve Ballinger, Anthony Barnett, Anita Bhalla, Rob Blackhurst, Mihir Bose, Jo Broadwood, Gordon Brown, Lucy Buckerfield, Ted Cantle, Douglas Carswell, Rosie Carter, Louise Casey, Ajay Chhabra, Trevor Chinn, Anthony Clavane, Linda Colley, Yvette Cooper, Alberto Costa, Linda Cowie, Jason Cowley, Brendan Cox, Shirley Cramer, Chris Creegan, Jon Cruddas, John Denham, Patrick Diamond, Andy Dixon, Bobby Duffy, Kezia Dugdale, David Edgar, Rakib Ehsan, Rokshana Fiaz, Daniel Finkelstein, Kate Ford, Rob Ford, Jonathan Freedland, Nus Ghani, Peter Gibson, Maurice Glasman, David Goodhart, Paul Goodman, Matthew Goodwin, Miranda Green, Ed Greig, Kevin

Hague, Daniel Hannan, Rabiha Hannan, Russell Hargrave, Gareth Harris, Ayesha Hazarika, Meg Henry, Henry Hill, Tom Holland, Tim Horton, Sunny Hundal, Dilwar Hussain, Ben Jackson, Howard Jackson, Sam Jacobs, Sajid Javid, Rachael Jolley, Andrew Kelly, Omar Khan, Sadiq Khan, Sara Khan, Jon Knight, Daniel Korski, Kwame Kweh-Armeh, David Lammy, Kim Leadbeater, Mark Leonard, Sonny Leong, Nick Lowles, Deborah Mattinson, Bharat Mehta, Binita Mehta, Ed Miliband, Tariq Modood, Avaes Mohammad, Marley Morris, Sarah Mulley, Alasdair Murray, Fraser Nelson, Hannah O'Rourke, Vinay Patel, Nick Pearce, Mark Perryman, Trevor Phillips, Jonathan Portes, Jake Puddle, Harvey Redgrave, Matthew Rhodes, Marcus Roberts, Ian Robinson, Heather Rolfe, Jonathan Rutherford, Jill Rutter, Shamit Saggar, Gurvinder Sandher, Ayesha Saran, Salma Shah, Frank Sharry, Ryan Shorthouse, Julie Siddiqi, Naved Siddiqi, Josh Simmons, Maria Sobolewska, Shailesh Solanki, Enver Solomon, Will Somerville, Tim Soutphommasane, Marc Stears, Andy Street, Gisela Stuart, Luke Tryl, Patrick Vernon, Burhan Wazir, Nat Wei, Justin Welby, Josh Westerling, Stewart Wood, Simon Woolley, Richard Wyn-Jones, Jon Yates, Robert Yates, Zehra Zaidi and Sabir Zazai.

Jonathan de Peyer at HarperNorth encouraged me to write this book and persuaded me too with his idea for its title. Thank you to the team at HarperNorth including Ben McConnell, Nick Fawcett, Jo Ireson, Ben Murphy and their colleagues for bringing it into the world. My colleagues, trustees and staff at British Future have been greatly supportive throughout.

Thank you to my mum and dad, without whom my Indian–Irish Evertonian perspective on being English and British would never have been possible, and to fellow travellers my twin sister Rohini, my now British–Canadian brother Ashok, and my sister Madhu. And thank you to my in-laws Kathy and Sam in Essex, who have given so much support and encouragement to our

Acknowledgements

family, for their willingness to allow the views from Essex to inform the conversation on Twitter and in this book.

This book is for Zarina and Jay, Sonny and Indira, and the futures that they can help to imagine and shape. Whatever challenges may lie ahead, I am always left more hopeful whenever I hear them talk about what identity means to them. The expectation of inclusion and commitment to making it a reality, which forms a starting point for many in their generation, can be a real force for positive change.

Thank you, above all, to Stacy, with love, for everything that should be recognised more.

Index

Index

Index

Harper
North

Book Credits

HarperNorth would like to thank the following staff
and contributors for their involvement in making
this book a reality:

Laura Amos
Hannah Avery
Fionnuala Barrett
Claire Boal
Caroline Bovey
Charlotte Brown
Sarah Burke
Alan Cracknell
Jonathan de Peyer
Anna Derkacz
Tom Dunstan
Kate Elton
Nick Fawcett
Simon Gerratt
Monica Green
Tara Hiatt
Graham Holmes
Ben Hurd

Patricia Hymans
Jo Ireson
Megan Jones
Jean-Marie Kelly
Ben McConnell
Ben Murphy
Alice Murphy-Pyle
Adam Murray
Genevieve Pegg
Agnes Rigou
Emma Rogers
Florence Shepherd
Zoe Shine
Eleanor Slater
Emma Sullivan
Katrina Troy
Phillipa Walker
Kelly Webster

For more unmissable reads,
sign up to the HarperNorth newsletter at
www.harpernorth.co.uk

or find us on Twitter at
@HarperNorthUK

**Harper
North**